CHANGE YOUR LIFE
CHANGE THE WORLD

CHANGE YOUR LIFE CHANGE THE WORLD

A SPIRITUAL GUIDE TO LIVING NOW

RYUHO OKAWA

IRH PRESS

The material in this book is selected from various talks given by
Ryuho Okawa to a live audience.

IRH PRESS

New York . Tokyo

Distributed by National Book Network Inc www.nbnbooks.com

Library of Congress Catalog Card Number: 2010931900

ISBN 13: 978-0-9826985-0-1

ISBN 10: 0-9826985-0-X

Printed in the United States of America

Cover Design © 2010 Yoori Kim
Book Design by Bookcraft Ltd
Cover Image © Dale Odell/Getty Images
Chapter Opener Graphic © Elena Andreeva – Fotolia.com

Contents

Preface

I WILL NEVER FORGET what happened to me on the memorable day of March 23, 1981.

It was a fine afternoon in early spring. The air was warm and the promise of the season was all around as I relaxed in a low chair, simply enjoying the day. All at once, an indescribable warmth welled up from deep inside my body. I instinctively knew that I was not alone and that another being was trying to communicate with me in some way. The feeling was so strong that I looked around immediately for something to write on. My hand fell on a card that lay on the table.

No sooner had I picked up the card and placed it in front of me, than the strangest thing imaginable happened. Of its own volition, without any conscious effort on my part, my right hand picked up a pencil and began to write. It felt absolutely as though someone else was controlling my hand. That presence wrote the words "Good News, Good News" in Japanese script. This was the way in which the first Divine Spirit to make contact with me announced his presence. I learned subsequently that the spirit's name is Nikko and that he was one of the six senior disciples of the thirteenth-century priest Nichiren.

The automatic writing continued and for perhaps ten days the messages I received all came from Nikko. Then, another being started to control my hand and to transmit messages. This was Nikko's master, Nichiren. At first, Nichiren did not make his true identity known to me and referred to himself by the name of one of his disciples. Before long, however, I was able to discern that the spirit was actually Nichiren himself.

I wondered why Nichiren had come to me. Perhaps, I thought, I was a student of the Nichiren sect of Buddhism in a past life. After communicating with Nichiren for some time, I learned that my father, Saburo Yoshikawa, in one of his own past incarnations, had been one of Nichiren's favorite disciples. This, I learned, was the connection that had led Nichiren to me.

Eventually, he began to contact me every day. In the initial stages, our communications were conducted almost entirely through automatic writing. My hand, uncontrolled by my will, would begin to write sentences and would continue to do so for some time. Nichiren's communications began toward the end of March 1981 and continued until the beginning of July.

It was around that time that I began to wonder if some other form of communication with Nichiren might be possible. Sudden and unexpected ideas would occasionally pass through my mind and I would hear silent voices speaking at the very core of my being, so it occurred to me that Nichiren and I might be able to communicate verbally.

Sure enough, the spirits that had communicated with me through automatic writing now began to speak to me by way of my own vocal chords. Now, instead of simply receiving the written messages, I was able to have oral discussions with the spirits. The situation would have seemed very odd to any onlooker because it would have seemed that I was talking to myself.

The importance of my experiences during that memorable first half of 1981 was that I gradually gained an understanding of the spiritual world that exists around us. At the time I began to receive messages, I thought I already had a good grasp of what lies beyond us after death, in the afterlife. But when my deeper abilities became apparent, when I could convey the words of spiritual agencies through speech, it caused me to make a one-hundred-and-eighty degree turn in my life and in my understanding.

You might ask what sort of special training I underwent in order to take part in the automatic writing and the direct, verbal communication that followed, but the truth is that it all happened quite naturally. I did not have to spend years meditating under a waterfall or retreat into the solitude of the mountains. Nor did I have to live for decades in a cave or take part in any specific techniques, special meditation, or complicated esoteric practices. All that was necessary was for me to look deep inside my mind and try to correct any wrong thoughts that lay there.

I was twenty-four years old at the time and was reviewing my life so far. In looking back, I realized I had already made many mistakes. I carefully examined these errors and repented the times I had thought or acted wrongly. In doing so, I was preparing myself to open the window of my soul.

Although I was still fairly young, I was somehow able to see quite clearly where I had gone wrong. I saw how, on so many occasions in my past, I had thought only about myself and believed I was the only person who mattered. Success, respect from others, a higher social status, and the acclaim of the world had been the only real components of my life. I found myself deeply embarrassed about the way I had lived up to that point.

As I continued the process of purifying and refining my heart in this way, although without realizing that this was what I was actually doing, I achieved the next necessary stage. A strong determination to devote my life to others sprang from the very depths of my being and became my state of mind.

When I asked myself to what extent I had put myself out for others or how much I had selflessly devoted myself to helping them, it became obvious that I could no longer go on living in the way I had. So absolute and overwhelming was the process I underwent, it could be said that, at only twenty-four, I experienced my first death. And it really *was* a death because I had laid to rest the false self I had been until that time.

Although the result of this change in my thinking gave me a strong desire to work on behalf of humanity, I had no idea how to proceed because I was only in my early twenties and lacked the life experience that could guide me to the concrete steps to take to fulfill my desire. I did not want to commit myself only to small acts of kindness because, as important as these are, I did not feel this was my true mission. I knew that I had to find a way to use my abilities and talents to the fullest and for the sake of others. But the burning question was, "How?" This was how my life review and my subsequent determination to express my gratitude and give to others in return for what I had been given represented a major turning point in my life.

It was then, that Nichiren began speaking to me. Any thought of publishing books or passing on Nichiren's words to others was far from my mind because the messages I was receiving seemed to be directed specifically at me. They were of a personal, rather than a public nature. My conversations with Nichiren took place at various times and in different places, for example, on the train to and from work or while I was on my lunch break.

When Nichiren contacted me while I was traveling on a train or in some other inconvenient place, I could obviously not speak out loud in reply, so I would generally write replies with my finger, as if it were a pen. This form of automatic writing, without the need for a pen and paper, worked well and allowed me to have all manner of conversations wherever I happened to be.

One of the phrases I remember most clearly from my early communications with Nichiren was "love, nurture, and forgive others." This was part of his response, in the form of automatic writing, when I asked him what my mission on Earth was – what I had been sent here to do. Nichiren told me that the words of his reply were to form the core of my philosophy. He did not go into detail, but added, "Believe in people, the world, and God." Thereafter, I contemplated these two messages frequently.

With regard to the message "believe in people, the world, and God," I think it can be explained as follows: "Believe in people" suggests that we should believe in the divine nature that sleeps within all individuals, and that the true essence of people is that they are children of God. "Believe in the world" springs from a belief in the divine nature of others. It means that we should not

11

look upon this world as evil. This world is a society created by children of God, and therefore it should be a utopian society. We need to create the kind of ideal world here on Earth that exists in the spirit world, in Heaven. This is how we need to think, as human beings, about this world and our society. Finally, "Believe in God" is the foremost, as well as the concluding, ultimate message, as this is the starting point of faith.

The message "love, nurture, and forgive others" is a teaching that everybody is capable of understanding. My personal philosophy is largely summed up in this message. It was six years, however, before it surfaced in my life in any public sense. In the intervening period, I considered these words very carefully, until it became clear to me that the phrase was connected with the developmental stages of love, a model that emerged from my thinking about the message. At that point, I wrote about it in the context of those stages in my book *The Laws of the Sun*.

Buddhism traditionally focuses on the stages and the development of enlightenment, while Christianity places its greatest importance on love. The search to achieve enlightenment and the posture of trying to offer love to people, are two approaches that appear to be quite different and it could be why the two religious movements have sometimes seemed incapable of merging. However, I discovered, to the contrary, that love and enlightenment are not only compatible ideas but are actually closely related to each other. The developmental stages of love reconciled the gap between these two ideas and showed that, at each level of love, there are corresponding stages of enlightenment, revealing a united model of Buddhist and Christian ideas.

I came to understand the developmental stages of love after contemplating Nichiren's message for six years. I realized that the first stage of human love is the type of love you feel for your parents, relatives, friends, and others you meet in the course of your life. This kind of love is for those you love quite naturally. I call this stage "fundamental love." For all people, this is the starting point of love.

I call the next stage "nurturing love." If you look at the world around you, you see numerous leaders. What is it that makes them so? The answer is that the best among them share a desire to nurture others; these are people who possess this greater, more highly developed form of love and make it their guiding principle. These are people who become leaders naturally. Leaders must not only love those whom it is natural to love, but due to their position, they must also love many others. They must give others the love that is known as leadership. Such people really do exist and they are outstanding individuals.

An even higher form of love, one that even the best leaders may not possess, is the stage I refer to as "forgiving love." This is love from a religious perspective. People may excel in earthly terms and nurture others, but to reach the stage of forgiving love requires more. It calls for a high degree of enlightenment, a great awakening. This spiritual awakening brings you into a state of mind close to that of God. It became obvious to me that this higher stage of love – forgiving love – exists, and that this love dissolves the need for distinction between good and evil in its purifying embrace. I came to know that this is the love that a truly religious or spiritual person possesses. These are the thoughts that occupied my heart after Nichiren started contacting me.

While I was receiving many spiritual messages from Nichiren and other Divine Spirits, I was holding down a full-time job at a large Japanese trading company where I was often quite overwhelmed by the work.

In the midst of such a frenetic life, I felt my heart waver many times, and despite the fact that I had already achieved what was clearly the first stage of enlightenment, I began to develop new worldly attachments. I think that part of the problem stemmed from my desire to achieve success in the company. It was still important to me to win recognition from others and be better than my colleagues. I strove relentlessly to become one of the elite, and as a result, created all kinds of grief for myself. When situations in my career did not go the way I wanted, my internal suffering increased. Numerous obstacles appeared that adversely affected the relationship I had with my boss and my colleagues. I had not encountered these kinds of problems in my student days and they created tremendous conflict in my heart.

In Japanese society, new recruits or employees are treated as if they are second-class, like privates in an army. The system of promotion by seniority is typical of all Japanese corporations, but I questioned the validity of assessing people simply on the grounds of the number of years they had worked for the same company. I found it very frustrating that an individual's worth should be judged in terms of years served rather than by their spiritual advancement, the state of their mind, or the level of their enlightenment.

Although we should not view or judge people as solely good or evil, when looked at through the spiritual eye, it cannot be denied that there are some people who have definite tendencies towards good, while others display a predisposition towards evil. When I looked through the eyes of God and in accordance with Truth, it became apparent to me that people with an inclination towards evil, who were motivated by egotism and displayed a strong desire to achieve in a material sense, were generally well received by the world. This astonished me.

As a result of these observations, I became determined to create a workplace in which employees were judged not by the length of their service but by the stage of development of their minds. It was my overriding hope and desire to see companies, organizations, and even the world based on true values.

Working in one of the leading trading companies in Japan, however, there seemed to be very little chance that I would be able to achieve my objectives. I decided that the only course of action left to me was to do my job to the best of my ability, while at the same time showing the people around me as much love as possible. This was not the sort of love that had any definite form but rather which supported others both openly and discreetly. I could do no more than this at the time.

During this period, I suffered significantly from conflicts caused by personal relationships. Even though I was able to open the window of my heart and to continue to speak with the Divine Spirits, as I had now been doing for some time, I encountered a variety of distractions. These often disturbed my equilibrium. Unfortunately, with my mind plagued by the emotions that ran through it, days sometimes passed without me being able to concentrate on my meditation.

When your mind is rocked by the desire for personal advancement and feelings, even of the most natural kind, towards the opposite sex, it is sometimes possible for the Devil to take this opportunity to attempt to enter your heart. Like many of the religious leaders of the past, I was forced to fight several Devils. Among the Devils that are famous from history are Lucifer, the ruler of Hell, and Beelzebub, the Devil who tempted Jesus during his forty days of solitude in the desert. Both these presences also came to attack me, in addition to another Devil of vast spiritual power, a well-known figure from esoteric Buddhism. One after another, I met these Devils face-to-face.

They would target my weakness and take advantage of my spiritual sensitivity, which is present in those who naturally possess spiritual abilities. So, on days when I was not feeling particularly well or when my mind was disturbed, the various Devils would appear and say things designed to turn me from my true, chosen path. When I had attachments, the Devils would do their best to amplify them, filling my mind with thoughts to which I was attached, and making it virtually impossible for me to think about anything else. As a result, I became exhausted and found myself unable to sleep at night.

As the situation continued, I had no option but to confront the Devils. Of course, I learned eventually that the true source of my distress lay within my own being. The Devils themselves were not outside of me, but were in my own heart. I realized that they had been able to creep in through the weaknesses that existed in my mind. Ultimately, it was my pride that had allowed them to exercise their power.

On many occasions, I weakened at the thought of following the path of Truth, and there were times when I wanted to rid myself of my ability to receive spiritual messages. It was in these moments of weakness that the Devils came to visit and taunt me. They told me that if I did not cease my communications with the Divine Spirits and abandon my enlightenment, if I would not abandon my plans to preach the Truth to others, I would never find happiness. I was falsely promised that if I discarded the Truth, abandoned my enlightenment, and gave up all thoughts of teaching others, I would soon achieve a promotion at work, enjoy a greater status, and earn a higher income. In these and many other ways, they attacked my weaknesses, constantly tempting me and trying to prevent my enlightenment with promises of worldly success.

During this period, I often found life difficult, but I remained true to my desire to improve myself. I had no way of knowing what would happen in the future. Even though I felt pressured to achieve personal success quickly, I could not see where it would lead. Although I had been given the message to love, nurture, and forgive people, I did not know how to apply the message in my own life. Nevertheless, I remained confident that my mission would be made clear to me in the fullness of time and that the day would arrive when I would be of genuine use to the world.

Until then, all I could do was to accept that I had started my journey as a person of ordinary ability. I must remain humble and continue to aim at self-improvement. I realized that it was wrong for me to think of myself as a special person just because I was able to communicate with the spirit world. I was an ordinary person and so I should do my best to live my life as an average citizen and a good member of society. I reasoned that, even if I lost my spiritual abilities and had my gift taken from me, I should still constantly strive to become the sort of individual whom others looked up to. I determined to try and make myself shine in the way I lived my everyday life, within the common and ordinary.

To achieve this, I consciously cast off all pretensions of greatness – the pride I had felt regarding my ability to communicate with the spirit world and also the idea that I must be someone very special. Instead I resolved to become simply the sort of person others would be happy to know. I would try to be like a refreshing spring breeze in May and become as near as I could get to a perfect example of an ordinary individual. For a while, to achieve this goal, I abandoned the spirit world and concentrated instead on re-examining myself and the way I was living, and checking that I was not mistaken in my actions.

The Devils had tried to gain control of my mind because of my feelings of superiority over others. I now know that Devils find it easy to enter into the hearts of people who seek psychic ability in order to become personally sublime. What ultimately drove them away in my case was not a stern rebuke or my powerful spiritual abilities. It was my constant resolve to make myself shine as a normal person. I constantly told myself: "There is nothing at all wrong with living an ordinary life. I will live a normal life and achieve accomplishments as a result of it. I don't even need to produce something great because something small will do. What is most important is to live the sort of life I can be proud of, to live in a way that other people would acknowledge and say, 'I am glad that we have someone like him.' This is the nature of the life I wish to live. From now on, I will build up my achievements gradually." I realized the importance of these words and began to carry them out in practice. It was then that the Devils left because they no longer had the power to accompany me. When I discovered how to shine like a warm light while living an ordinary life, the Devils finally left me alone.

I am sure that many of you reading this are interested in spiritual matters. Some of you may already possess spiritual abilities. If this is the case, you must not see these as a way to become extraordinary. You must realize that to do so will put you on the edge of a fearful precipice. A longing to become a famous or extraordinary human being brings with it a craving for prestige, and thoughts of this sort provide food for the Devils. When you know you have made these mistakes, strive for an ordinary life – seek light within that ordinariness. In other words, start afresh as a normal person.

It is important to ask yourself: If I should suddenly be stripped of my spiritual abilities, would I still be an admirable and good individual? When my days in this world are over, will my life have been meaningful? If the answer to both questions is a truthful "yes," you have learned how to overcome the Devil who finds a home within you.

In my confrontation with the Devils, I spent almost six years engaged in strict training of my soul. I struggled to polish myself, always by way of a normal and unassuming life. Then, as I approached the age of thirty, something quite extraordinary started to develop from my ordinary accomplishments.

Throughout this period, my father, Saburo Yoshikawa, was a great source of strength to me and worked hard at compiling the spiritual messages I received. He arranged them into book form and found a publisher for them. We began to publish a compilation every two months. First came *The Spiritual Messages of Nichiren*, followed by *The Spiritual Messages of Kukai*, and then *The Spiritual Messages of Jesus Christ*.

Despite the successful publication of the messages, this was an extremely painful time for me. I had reached the point in my career at which I was approaching middle management. The path to future promotion lay before me. I retained a strong ambition to advance in the business world and to achieve personal success as a result, but I also realized that I could not allow things to go on the way they were. I had to find some way of accomplishing the special mission I knew I had been given in this world. The two paths were not compatible and they caused a conflict within me.

Part of the problem was fear of the unknown. Even during the time I was receiving messages from the Divine Spirits, I struggled with the problem of how to go about spreading this knowledge to the world and to create some kind of organization based on all I had been told.

The situation came to a head shortly before my thirtieth birthday. The Divine Spirits had been talking to me for six years and the message I received from them at this pivotal juncture of my life was, "Now is the time to move."

Hearing this and taking note of it, I finally made up my mind to hand in my notice to the company for which I had worked. I was determined to stand on my own feet and live in the Truth.

Up until that time, I had intended to continue working to earn a living while simultaneously carrying out my spiritual activities. I came to the conclusion, however, that I did not need an income. In fact, I did not need anything. From that point on, my mind was clear. I did not care what happened to me as I dedicated my life to spreading the Truth. It did not even matter to me if I should lose my very life.

When I left my career behind, I had enough money saved to support myself for only one year. I was resolute, however, that even if I starved once that money ran out, I would simply try to do what I could in the time available. I would do what I wanted to do and I would avoid worrying about what would happen in the future. All I knew for certain was that this was the course I needed to take. I no longer found it possible to avoid what I knew was my duty and my vocation. I wanted to embark fully on the path of Truth and walk straight along that path. My career and my reputation were suddenly of no importance, and I did not care if people thought I was bad or mad. Henceforth, I might be referred to as a guru, or I might be called crazy, but it didn't matter. I gave up everything and I was even prepared to surrender my earthly life.

This moment marked the birth of Ryuho Okawa. Until this time, I had a different name written in the official family register, but I decided to cast that old name aside along with everything else and to live my future life under my holy name of Ryuho Okawa.

I had undergone my first "death" at the age of twenty-four. At the age of thirty, I experienced my second "death" as I cast off everything belonging to my past. In addition to leaving my work, I broke off many of my personal relationships; I stopped seeing my old friends, my former colleagues, my superiors, and the people who had worked under me. I abandoned my old life entirely and was also content to give up all hope for the future. I discarded everything and started afresh. With this mindset and to fulfill my mission, I set out to create an organization that would become Happy Science.

Discarding everything in this way, including myself, allowed me to be truly reborn. The first few months were hard because I had no income and no prospects. All I had to keep me going were the words of the Divine Spirits and my own determination. By getting rid of my old self, however, I came into possession of the key to a great step forward. And having "died" twice, I was no longer scared of anything. Those who are not afraid to abandon everything they own have nothing left to fear. Even now, as I am preaching the Truth, I am quite prepared to lose everything if necessary and to stand empty-handed once again. I remain ready to start once more from the beginning, and as a result, I have no fear.

Achieving this state of mind is the first step in becoming an awakened one, someone who has attained enlightenment. Shakyamuni Buddha went through this experience, and although the details of his life and the environment in which he lived were different from my own, our minds were in the same state. We both determined to live for the sake of Truth and we both discovered our true selves and were awakened to a spiritual perspective of life.

It remains my dearest wish that many more people will have this experience in the future.

It is my intention to continue to preach and spread the Truth and I am confident that these activities will expand both in quality and quantity. As my work becomes more intense, it is inevitable that I will be misunderstood and mocked. In fact, there are already people who claim our work at Happy Science is undertaken for the sake of personal glory and financial gain. People who make such accusations probably do so because the criticisms they voice actually refer to the state of their own minds. Having died twice, I remain unperturbed by their criticism. This is thanks to an indomitable spirit that can only be experienced by casting away the old self, undergoing that necessary "death." This state of mind can only be discovered by those who have cast everything aside, including their pride and their future.

I am not remotely interested in personal glory, nor do I crave worldly success. I content myself with simply doing what needs to be done and what I want to do. I am tilling the soil. If people accuse me of doing it the wrong way, I do not care. I will continue my mission until every inch of earth has been ploughed.

I will remain happy as long as I can live for others. I am devoted to people alive in the world today and those who are to come. If possible, I would like to be able to leave something enduring, something that will still be of use to people two or three thousand years into the future. I want to create something that will act as nourishment to the soul of many. I remain filled with a wish to become like the cool water of a desert oasis – water that is inexhaustible, no matter how much is drawn off. It is my ardent desire to become a fount and source of the spiritual laws.

It does not matter in the least that I started my journey as an ordinary person. It is my mission to continue spreading the Truth to the world at large as long as I live. No doubt the accumulation of ordinary efforts will be transformed into an extraordinary love that will rise majestically and will shine out across the world when I finish my mission on Earth. I began my task with a pure mind and that is how I intend to finish it.

CHAPTER 1

Unlocking the Door to
A New World

TO BEGIN OUR QUEST, we need to contemplate the meaning of life and the truth of who we really are. Have you ever stopped to look at yourself – at the very essence of your personal identity? You probably consider yourself to be a fully independent entity, a single individual among countless others in the world. It seems logical and right to assume that this is the case because we have separate bodies and each of us has a totally unique identity. As sensible as this assumption may seem, however, I want you to consider whether this way of viewing yourself in isolation is really a complete and truly fulfilling outlook on life and whether it is even correct.

In the world of religion and myth, and from a time so long ago we cannot know its beginning, there has been an enduring belief. People from all over our planet have told and retold stories about a huge tree that exists in the universe. Although this tree has many names and different cultures have depicted it in various ways, it was deeply important to all our ancestors, wherever they lived. Scandinavians called it the World Tree, and the ancient Mesopotamians called it the Tree of Life. It features in the mythologies of ancient China, India, and Mesoamerica. No matter by what name it has been called, the Cosmic Tree stands at the very center of human religious belief and countless millions have revered it through many millennia.

You could take the world's most advanced telescope and gaze at the heavens until you had observed every part of the material universe, but you could never see the great Cosmic Tree through the telescope's eyepiece. The Cosmic Tree can only be perceived with your spiritual eye.

From its massive, ancient trunk, the branches of the Cosmic Tree stretch out in all directions forming a canopy that inhabits all parts of creation in the universe. A branch of the Cosmic Tree reaches out to Earth. When seen through your spiritual eye, this massive branch looks like the huge trunk of a tree, with more branches that extend to connect all creation on Earth. The name of this immense tree is El Cantare and it is the origin of all life on Earth. What is more, all spiritual energy flows through and from El Cantare.

As the boughs of El Cantare extend farther and farther from the trunk, they divide into smaller branches. The many branches springing from El Cantare represent the different religious and ethnic groups that have flourished in various places in the world throughout history. Each branch may represent a new country, but it is equally likely that it extends beyond nationhood to include various regions, for example areas in Asia or Europe. In other cases, particular branches extend throughout the world to various ethnic groups where people can be found who share a particular way of thinking.

The differences between the groups are, in reality, just differences in religious beliefs and practices. Religion has existed throughout time as the fundamental basis of culture and civilization. Each ethnic group was originally formed from the followers of one of the many religious leaders who appeared in the world and preached new messages, but all come from the same source. Over perhaps thousands of years, a particular ethnic group develops specific practices and characteristics. Individuals reincarnate in the same civilization several times and repeatedly experience the culture of that specific region.

This view of life may seem extraordinary, but it represents the ultimate Truth of existence. It is quite different from the worldview you acquired in school or even that you absorb from reading books and magazines, or watching television. Many people think of themselves as living their own lives, responsive only to their own will, and divorced from their fellow human beings. Although individual souls exist independently, they cannot avoid also being part of the greater whole and all are attached to the great Tree of Life. The ultimate Truth is that human beings are reborn on many occasions in an endless cycle of reincarnation within the structure of the Tree of Life.

Once you begin to accept this as the true perspective on life and reality, your attitude towards many situations will reverse completely. At the moment, you may be looking at yourself and thinking, "But this is my real self. This individual who exists now, who has my name and personality, is my real and only self." If you are thinking this, you may not have perceived the other world, the world of spirit, and you may not have heard of individuals who have visited that realm and returned to tell about it. Like many people who have not developed an awareness of the spirit world, you may have no idea what happened to you before you were born into this life or where you will go when it is over.

This is all quite normal and understandable on the material plane we presently inhabit. We seldom, if ever, gain any other view of life, even in our education systems. Although we can learn a great deal from the experiences we have in the world, we need something further to assist us in seeing in a different way. Only religions that offer a correct perspective and a true understanding can teach us the real and most rewarding view of life and the world.

So, despite what seems apparent, don't be fooled into thinking that your physical body as it exists at this moment in time is your true self. You are merely a traveler who happens to be temporarily visiting this little planet we call Earth, which is really only a tiny spot in an infinitely vast universe. As a visitor you will remain here for a few decades and then return to the true reality of the spirit world. The whole purpose of living an earthly existence is to learn new lessons and to gain knowledge.

Soul Siblings and Reincarnation

Now, visualize the boughs of the Tree of Life dividing into smaller branches and the branches splitting to create twigs in full leaf. Looking closely, you see that each twig has six leaves attached to it. Think of every group of six leaves as representing a single life form – the soul. We can refer to the leaves in such a grouping as "soul siblings."

Under most circumstances, a group of soul siblings is responsive to one core soul. This represents the central point, the command center of the soul, which shares its essence with five other soul siblings. All the soul siblings experience life, one after another. Each takes its turn at being born on Earth, where it lives out a material existence in human form. Each soul sibling carries with it about one-sixth of the energy of the soul when it is born into a human body. While you are living in the material world, the rest of your soul, represented by your five soul siblings, remains in the spirit world, and one member of your soul sibling group acts as a guardian spirit. So, even though it may sometimes seem that you are alone, this is never the case.

After a lifetime of spiritual training on Earth, the soul sibling returns to the spirit world with a new personality gained during its life. When soul siblings return to the spirit world after death, most tend to retain the appearance they had during their time as corporeal beings. The experience gained by each soul sibling on Earth is not restricted to a single lifetime. Each soul sibling returns, time and again, reincarnated into different lives, thereby acquiring different personalities. When the soul siblings eventually come together, however, they still represent one complete soul. Each soul sibling knows that it is one component of the whole and that it and the other siblings together form one unique human soul.

The soul therefore has a multitude of memories and experiences supplied by each component part overlapping and converging. As an example, and using Japanese eras, let us say you were born into three periods: the Heian Period (794–1185), the Kamakura Period (1185–1333), and the Edo Period (1603–1867). You would retain the life experiences from your reincarnations into the world in all these periods of history. In those lifetimes, you would have encountered many different circumstances, met countless other incarnated souls, and played various roles in the earthbound incarnations that are part of the development of the soul.

Each person who is alive now will gain new experiences in the present era of the twenty-first century. You will study new material, encounter new situations, and eventually return to the spirit world with renewed nourishment gained from your earthly lives. Once you are reintegrated there, your soul siblings will share your new memories and gain from your experience. Within the entire soul are memories that go way back into much earlier lives and eras, but such remembrances gradually fade away as each soul sibling is born time and again. Each new life refreshes the soul's pool of experience as new knowledge and experience are gained.

The concept of the soul "leaves" on the Tree of Life might be difficult to grasp at the moment because you look at the world only from the perspective of your present earthly life. To understand and to gain a new perspective on your life, focus your mind on a single twig of the Tree of Life, where six leaves grow. Think of yourself as one of these leaves.

Leaves flourish and grow, before turning red, orange, or yellow then brown and eventually falling. At a human level, this is equivalent to passing through the peak of life, old age, and death. As the years go by, you think, "These days I am less vigorous. My body is weaker and my back is bent." You may notice that you have more wrinkles, begin to lose your hair, and are more susceptible to sickness. This is the time you become like the withered brown leaf. And as surely as the leaf is eventually detached from the tree by the late autumn winds, so you will eventually leave your human body behind and return to the spirit world. Fallen leaves carpet the forest floor, passing their nutrients back to the soil, where they are reabsorbed by the tree, offering nourishment to new leaves. This is the life of the individual when seen from the perspective of the Tree of Life. The analogy is sound because, as a result of your many incarnations, you amass experiences that nourish and feed the Tree of Life.

SOULS CONNECTED BY SPIRITUAL BONDS

I want to carry our contemplation of the Tree of Life a little further. I have explained that the six leaves that grow on a single twig of the tree represent your soul group, which consists of you and your five soul siblings. Close to you are other twigs that developed from the same branch as yours. The souls occupying these adjacent twigs are related souls, having developed from the same common branch. The souls adjacent to you came into existence at about the same time as you did and they have close connections with you. For this reason, they are often called soul mates. Even though these nearby souls are not your soul siblings, they are part of the group with whom you will always undergo soul training on Earth.

You will generally be born into the same periods as your soul mates. In life, they will become your family members, more distant relatives, good friends, or perhaps colleagues you meet on a regular basis. This applies to your own parents, brothers and sisters, grandparents, children, and grandchildren. It also applies to friends with whom you share a commonality and a destiny, as well as to people with whom you feel an affinity for no particular reason.

People with whom you are now associated at many levels have been important to you in past incarnations, and you have shared many different relationships with them. For example, even though you may be husband or wife to a particular individual now, the two of you could have been father and daughter in a previous incarnation. Sometimes an older brother you love dearly was your father in a past life, or the aunt for whom you feel a special love and who has always offered you useful advice may have been your mother at some time in the past. Even those who become your rivals could once have been your dearly loved brothers or sisters.

Your relationships with those who are part of your spiritual group will vary from lifetime to lifetime as you repeatedly reincarnate. You and your soul mates undertake your life training through many kinds of associations and relationships. In trying to understand the meaning of your life, it is essential to contemplate your existence at a much deeper level than is generally done in our material world.

These days, with better nutrition and health care, people often live as long as eighty or ninety years, leading to rich experiences across a long period of time. Under such circumstances, changes in relationships are inevitable. As circumstances alter, however, there are always going to be people around whom you recognize as soul mates. Fate is not something that is fixed or unchangeable. So even if specific relationships with family members, friends, or business associates collapse or fade away, there will always be soul mates or soul friends with whom you have special ties, and they will appear among the new relationships you make. These soul mates and soul friends will step up to help you when needed.

Today, in the unsettled flow of modern society, there are many divorces and remarriages especially in Europe and North America. The concept of a single thread of fate connecting husband and wife for all eternity may make little sense. In Christian societies, when two people marry, they pledge that no one will ever separate a relationship that has been sanctified by God. They may feel guilty when things go wrong and they find it necessary to break the oath and to remarry. The Church cannot rescue believers from the feelings of guilt that arise. As a result, many individuals search for a different perspective and try to ensure their religious salvation through other means.

Spiritual counselors and other kinds of practitioners offer consultations to advise such people on marital matters and to answer questions about whether their marriage partners are connected to them by fate. Many counselors offer readings relating to past lives in order to establish whether their new partners may have been close to them in past incarnations. When spiritual counselors say that the potential marriage partners were connected to each other in previous incarnations, the information serves to lessen their feelings of guilt. In fact, there are many instances in which these past life relationships were significant to the parties concerned. Even if you are forced by circumstance to go through divorce and remarriage, please do not torment yourself about the fact. The person you subsequently marry more than likely had a spiritual tie with you in previous lives.

In every era in which you incarnate in the world, a number of closely related souls come to Earth at the same time as you and share your spiritual training. The population of the world now numbers more than six billion individuals and it is growing towards seven billion. It is almost certain that people who were born in different eras of the past are being born simultaneously at this time. Among these people, there are many who belong to your spiritual group, that is, those from nearby twigs of the Tree of Life.

You may meet one or several people during your life who especially captivate you and lift your heart. These sorts of relationships not only develop between men and women but also between people of the same gender. You may develop such a close affinity that they feel as though they are family members, even though in a relationship sense they are not. Some friendships are so strong they seem to be destined. You may meet a special person with whom you actively choose to spend the rest of your life. These are the people who have a spiritual connection with you. If you reflect on your own life, it will be obvious that soul mates do exist.

There is apt to be a group of about twenty to thirty people close to you with whom you have very special spiritual ties. This group of people will most likely determine the happiness and sorrow of your life. In almost all cases, these are the people you are supposed to meet in this lifetime because you previously made plans to meet them in your present incarnation.

During your life, people will appear whom you are absolutely required to meet because what they offer you is part of the training of your soul. You may encounter these people once or on many occasions during your time here. Some of these individuals will treat you with the warmest kindness, but others will be less appealing and will provide you with some of the trials that are inevitable in life. Nevertheless, these are people you simply have to experience. Think of your life as a workbook that is assigned to you. Meeting with particular individuals is part of your workbook, so that you can resolve issues you had with them in previous lives. You carried over these assignments from past incarnations.

As an example, in a past life, you may have had a great relationship with someone as a parent and child, brother and sister, or husband and wife. Yet, in the course of your life, something happened that caused you to hate each other. In such cases, it is vital that you and that person meet again on the earthly plane, though in a different sort of association, to test how you will treat each other now.

Where love–hate problems arise in relationships, especially when the connections are with people who have a deep influence on your life, these are most likely difficulties that have been carried over from a past life. Each problem from the workbook of life is something you must solve, and it is part of God's plan for you. Please do not assume that suffering is simply a matter of bad luck. It is far better to approach difficulties as tests from your workbook of life rather than as random chance events. Many things that happen to you occur because they are necessary and inevitable.

You and your soul mates have come together in countless periods and regions, especially in the present era when new teachings of the Truth are available. You were all born into numerous civilizations in the past, including ones that have become mere legends in modern times. You have met each other repeatedly in different situations and your relationships to each other have altered. You switched genders and roles within families across countless centuries and now you have come face-to-face with the same individuals in your present life. Within the vast sea of life, there have been and will be many dramas, but I want you to know that you have a deep connection with the people you meet.

Now that you are aware of this Truth, I ask that when you meditate, you think of a person that has made a strong impression on your life and contemplate the possibility that this specific individual has a deep spiritual connection with you and may be tied to you as a soul mate.

OVERCOMING HATRED

Many people follow the Western value of individualism, believing that people who compete and win in life are somehow superior. This brings a "defeat or be defeated" attitude. Such competition can lead to your mind seesawing between a heavenly state and a hellish state, depending on the outcome in each competitive encounter.

When you find yourself stuck in this situation, I would like you to think again about the great Tree of Life, visualizing it spreading through space and extending its branches far beyond the realms of Earth, stretching on to far-flung planets where other life forms exist. This single massive tree ultimately connects all of the souls in creation throughout the universe. You may win or lose in our competitive world, but remember that the people who are your opponents now are not your absolute enemies or rivals. These are people you have met many times before across a host of lifetimes. In a spiritual sense, everyone is connected by way of the Tree of Life.

This is why I am teaching everyone to love each other. I am saying, "Please love one another. You must love one another." You are not strangers. Every single person is associated, and everyone's life energy connects to the same spiritual root.

When individualism becomes overly dominant, it causes people to develop excessive envy, jealousy, possessiveness, and ultimately, hatred. Such behavior goes against the laws of life, and it will ultimately be judged as a negative deed that requires self-reflection.

The people with whom you share close relationships are all connected to you on the same branch of the Tree of Life. It is a sin to hate or loathe individuals with whom you come into contact because, in so doing, you damage or even sever a branch that is connected to the same bough as yours.

This is the message I want to impart: Stop hurting each other. Stop speaking ill of others. Don't be jealous of those around you; instead, bless them. In this way, you develop your own soul.

Jealousy and hatred exist as an opposition to love, but the difficulties that arise as a result of wrong thinking can be overcome by being aware of the Truth. You compete with others and grow jealous of them because you see yourself as being totally separate from them, but these same individuals are actually your soul mates.

So much hatred and conflict arises today due to differences in ethnicity or religion, but this is only because people do not fully understand the Truth. This is why contemplation of the Tree of Life is so important. If we come to realize absolutely that we are all born of branches that form part of the same tree, war and strife will disappear from our world. The purpose of our movement at Happy Science is to teach this to everybody. By so doing, we are trying to bring peace and abundance to the world and unite the world as one.

MATERIAL VS. SPIRITUAL PERSPECTIVE

Today, many individuals tend to analyze everything from a narrow perspective, much like an ant walking around a tiny patch of earth and trying to observe the whole world. This takes place in education, in business, and in the mass media. Because people fail to see the greater perspective, they adhere to a value system that is based only on the material world and base their thoughts on logic amassed only from the specialized knowledge of their limited earthly vision.

For instance, there are intellectually motivated doctors who become fixed on materialism. There are also teachers who believe they cannot participate in any religious activity or mention anything about faith, simply because they are public workers. In addition to imparting material knowledge, those employed to educate should be "teachers of souls." These professionals are not alone in denying faith in their occupational roles. Many other people in today's society are engaged in numerous activities and actions that are wrong according to the true morals of life, the laws of life, and the ethics of good and evil that are based on the Truth. If people could take a much broader perspective of the world and indeed the entire universe, they would be able to perceive the Truth.

Success in the material world is different from what is considered success in the spirit world. To achieve spiritual success, you must have a firm understanding of the Truth and have an unfaltering pillar of true faith within you. If you consider only your material success or failure in this world, without having genuine faith, you will never be able to gain true success. You can become an expert in a subject, acquire an abundance of knowledge, and celebrate excellent achievements in this world, but if all of this does not correspond to the fundamental faith, you will not be able to achieve true happiness.

As one example, consider a person who has become extremely famous as an author of novels about violence and murder. Let us suppose that the books become long-time bestsellers all around the world and the television series based on them are wildly popular. The person in question might be highly regarded in society, but spiritually he is likely to suffer significantly. It is possible that such an individual may experience pain in a world much like the one he has created in his novels. This is because the writer had such an extreme interest in murder and violence, plotting for his books about how to kill people or lure them into deadly traps. The soul of a person who thinks about such things all the time is inevitably destined to spend a significant time in Hell. Therefore, no matter how highly esteemed individuals may be in this world, the respect and adulation they achieve does not guarantee that they will immediately return to Heaven.

The same is true of academic achievement. Those who receive good grades in education, who attend the best schools, and who go to the best universities are often considered winners in this world. Such people may find employment with top-notch companies or go on to join the government. They are often considered the most prominent people in society. If we look at such people from a spiritual perspective, however, there may actually be many aspects about them that are not so great. Unless they also learned true spiritual values and worked hard to improve their outlook on life, while also cultivating feelings of love for others, they may end up suffering in their afterlife in the spirit world. This applies equally to success in the business world, defined as the level of prestige of one's company, and to the success of high social status, such as that of a lawyer or physician. I urge you not to be deluded by the false value systems that are so in evidence in measures of success in this world. These judge people solely based on their social status, the name of their company, or even their technical skills.

It is necessary to look carefully at everything at all times to determine whether you are seeing the world from the perspective of Truth. You should always consider whether faith precedes all other values in your decisions and perceptions – that the precedence of faith is the basis of your life. If you lose this necessary spiritual perspective, you can become separated from the Tree of Life, and may suffer the torment of Hell as a result. For this reason, please think again about the precedence of the Truth and of faith over the false values of this world.

THE COMPENSATIONS FOR CHOOSING FAITH

In order to live with the precedence of faith, you need to be aware of the law of compensation, a law that rules our lives. The word "compensation" is often used in phrases such as "compensation for peace" and "to pay a certain amount of compensation." It infers an equivalent value or cost. Observations and experience show that there is a certain compensation you need to pay in life. This is the law of compensation.

In the law of compensation lies the idea of making an effort to accomplish something. In this case, the "cost" is the effort you make. There are, however, also things you must be willing to abandon. According to the law of compensation, you must give up things that are less significant to your life in order to achieve something significant. For example, if you wish to graduate from university with good grades, find a good job, and be successful in society, you cannot spend all your time gambling. This might be fine if you intend to live the life of a professional gambler or if you want to gamble moderately, work moderately, and live a moderate life. If you have high aspirations and need to concentrate on achieving them, however, you must give up your gambling activities, even if you enjoy them.

Understanding the concept of giving up something to gain something else is also important in personal relationships. It is quite possible to love more than one person and to be involved in several romantic attachments at the same time. Although you may think you could be happy receiving love from a number of partners, the joy of this situation will be short-lived. It will most likely lead to misery. It is almost certain that you will have to pay the debt of compensation in the form of jealousy, deceit, and self-destructive outcomes. Then, at a certain point, you will be obliged to abandon what you had and experience even more suffering.

No area of life is immune from the law of compensation. You may own many books on subjects you want to learn about, but it is wholly impossible to master them all. If you cannot accomplish everything with your current abilities, you must let something go. You need to decide what you are going to concentrate on first and master that before you attempt to move on. Later, if you are capable of more, move on to the next subject and look at that. Nobody can achieve everything at the same time. This is an important lesson to keep in mind.

Throughout life, there are times when you have to choose what to keep and what to abandon. Sometimes you will have to pay compensation in the form of effort or devotion, and at other times the compensation lies in letting go of what you would rather keep. If you think you can gain a double advantage in a certain situation, you will probably be wrong and will eventually have to abandon something. Unless you pay the compensation, you cannot attain what you most desire. In this sense, abandoning your attachments is another way for you to attain happiness.

In addition to saying that if you want to gain something, you also need to abandon something, the law of compensation states that nothing is gained without perseverance and devotion. It follows that what you pay or exert is equivalent in value to what you gain.

In the end, the best compensations in life are those you receive for what you pay out for faith. Giving up something for the sake of God and what you know to be true means you will gain the greatest blessings in the next world. You may sometimes have to make a great effort, devote yourself fully, and give up a great deal for faith. There will be times when you have to abandon desires and let go of things you would have longed for if you relied entirely on your material instincts. You will certainly be called on to abandon apparently important ambitions for faith, but in the end many of these will turn out to be transitory and of little worth, whereas faith endures.

Living with faith as your priority means abandoning something for faith. Ask yourself what compensations you have paid to put your faith into practice so far. What have you done in this lifetime to strengthen your faith and to act on the conviction that faith surpasses all, that it is the most important and valuable consideration? You can be certain that your future will correspond to the compensations you have made. The balance will add up perfectly on both sides of the ledger, and there are no exceptions to this rule.

Although giving up something for faith may seem in opposition to the values of the material world, you are improving your soul and embarking on a path that ensures your soul's success. Suffering through many hardships and ordeals in this world actually means that your soul has been training hard. The presence of suffering also indicates that you are, in fact, one of the elite, one of the chosen souls. The people we generally think of as the elite, those who cruise through life with everything going well and with material success on all sides, are not truly the elite at all. The true elite are the people who overcome many trials in life, who suffer persecution, illness, financial struggles, or other hardships and who manage to grasp true faith as a result of their experiences. What is more, the people who make an effort to help and save others, despite the difficulties they are facing, are the ones God has chosen. They are truly elite souls.

How much of the world's material values can you abandon and choose to live in Truth? This is the most crucial point of the law of compensation. This is what Shakyamuni Buddha and Jesus Christ preached. They both taught that we should rid ourselves of the possessions and values that are considered important only on an earthly level. This is the law of compensation. Those who have an attachment to the material things of this world sink by the very weight of their attachments. Those who remain unattached to worldly considerations and live a life with spiritual eyes – the eyes of God – will without doubt one day sit close to God.

Once you start living with a true outlook of the world and see it from the perspective of the larger universe, you may regularly find yourself in conflict with the values of the material world. In the economy and in government, in law and in education, in family problems or in your views on marriage and relationships, your values may often clash with those of society.

Even if you become very successful in the world, you can only live a matter of decades at best and rarely more than a century. If the success you achieve goes against the laws of the universe, it will become an obstacle to the overall success of the Tree of Life. Material success that contradicts the natural, cosmic laws of life will dissolve into bitter emptiness. This is why having a foundation of understanding the Truth and having faith in it are of the utmost importance.

As a religious leader, in order to open the doors to everyone's happiness in the future, I am looking out beyond the present era, forward into the twenty-second, twenty-third, twenty-fifth, thirtieth, fortieth, fiftieth centuries, and even beyond. Contemplating an era very far ahead, I feel that we need to build a society with a solid foundation of Truth and faith, a society in which people recognize the Truth and live it with a faith in God. A solid foundation of the Truth and the precedence of faith are vital to creating a world filled with happiness.

I hope with all my heart that you will shine brightly as a part of the Cosmic Tree and that you will have the great courage to live a life of faith.

CHAPTER 2

Eternal Life and Reincarnation

YOUR HAPPINESS OR UNHAPPINESS on Earth depends in large measure on what foundation for living you create and the way you strive to build an elegant and attractive building upon it. There are any numbers of religions and spiritual teachers in the world, and thus, many teachings and suggested paths to enlightenment. There is one important Truth above everything that any of the teachings may tell you, however. It is that the greatest blessing of all is to be awakened to the fact that each and every person in the world has been endowed with eternal life.

Some people have no idea where we came from or what will happen to us after we die, and in the main, they prefer not to think about it. They assume they arrived in the world by chance and they think their identities and life circumstances are equally haphazard. Sadly, many people operate from this perspective for their entire lives. These people have never been fortunate enough to learn the fundamental Truth that all of us have eternal lives. I feel great compassion for such individuals because their time on Earth will simply represent days, months, and years of suffering and pain. They end life feeling sad and lonely, miserable and exhausted. They are often unaware of the many opportunities available and rarely try to expand their potential. It is paradoxical that, despite their belief that life is one long round of misery, many such people also live in great fear of death, thinking that it represents the end of their existence.

Fortunately, there are other individuals who adopt a different, more positive perspective on the meaning of life. Although these people recognize that death appears to be an end when viewed from a purely physical perspective, they can also readily accept that the death of the body is not the end of real life, that people have eternal lives. When we grow old, we become more susceptible to illness and infirmity and it isn't as easy to get about. It is inevitable that our bodies eventually wear out. But this is only how it appears physically, and the truth is that long before you were born into an earthly life, your soul existed as a child of God, and when death comes to take you from the world, you are not simply extinguished. Your soul continues to exist. People who know this Truth are aware that the true essence of a person is the soul and that this entity lives forever, incarnating continuously between Heaven and Earth. Your true essence, the divine nature within you, was already shining with divine light when you were in Heaven, but your incarnations on Earth will provide your soul with experiences to make it shine even brighter. Because they are aware that life on Earth is a form of education for our souls, they are able to see the great value in spending many decades living on Earth.

THE RISKS YOU TOOK FOR THE SAKE OF LIFE

Birth into this world is a dangerous gamble that involves many risks. From our serenity in Heaven, we watch as our parents are born and then eventually meet and marry. We wait for our future mother to become pregnant and then, in the ninth week and after great preparation, the soul enters the chosen mother's womb. For the rest of the pregnancy, the soul remains within the mother's body, confined and restricted. During this period, any number of accidents or medical problems can arise, some of which can result in a miscarriage. But, no matter what befalls the waiting soul, we must patiently experience the terror of uncertainty regarding our future.

Of course, the souls that begin the journey into life understand that there is a possibility that they might not come to birth and they also know that half the souls fail in their endeavor to live good, honest, and truthful lives and pass temporarily into fearful realms in Hell, where they might spend from a few decades to several centuries. Each soul is well aware of this risk and yet a great number of souls aspire to be reborn into the world and to face the doubt and uncertainty of the journey.

Birth into this world is similar to the sort of danger that Kukai and his companions faced when they set off for China. During the period of the Tang Dynasty in China (618–907), Japanese Buddhist monks crossed the turbulent seas to look more closely at the teachings of the Buddha, which had been studied more fully in that country. One of the monks was a man named Kukai. Kukai was born around 774, and in addition to being a monk, he was an engineer, scholar, poet, and calligrapher. With some of his colleagues, Kukai sailed from Japan to China on one of four small boats carrying naval envoys, but the journey was very hazardous and only two of the boats arrived; the others sank or were lost at sea.

The monks did not need to risk their lives in this way, but they did so willingly out of their aspiration for learning the Truth from Buddhist teachings. The only chance they would have to return to Japan after their studies was if more naval envoys managed to make the journey safely at some time in the future. In fact, Kukai and his associates were well aware that they might never see their homeland again. Despite these risks, they viewed the journey as a precious experience. It was an opportunity to better understand the Buddha's teachings, and they hoped, eventually to return to Japan to pass on the teachings to their fellow countrymen and women. It was a spiritual mission of great worth; accomplishing it would give the soul a priceless experience.

Before we are born on Earth, our souls live in Heaven, in serenity and happiness. Despite this, we willingly dare to take the hazardous journey into life, facing all the challenges this involves. We enter life courageously, not knowing if we will return safely or will have to endure decades of suffering. We do so because, like Kukai, we are sure that the result of our risk will be worthwhile in terms of our own soul's progress and also in the hope that we can be of great use to others.

At the moment we pass through our mother's body and are born, we forget who we were in our previous incarnations. We may have been a great religious leader or an artist, a peasant, or a king. Once born again, however, we forget whatever previous experience we gained and have to start over from scratch, dealing with the hard knocks of life, just like any other individual. Before being born into the world, we choose our own parents and make a pact with them to be born someday as their child. This pact with our parents is also forgotten, as are the agreements made with soul siblings before the journey began. In a new incarnation, we will not usually even recognize our soul mates and will be completely unaware of the bonds we formed with them previously. All souls, regardless of the lives lived before, must go through this journey of self-discovery. When we enter this world, we begin our soul's spiritual training on Earth completely anew; it is a new beginning, a new start from point zero.

When we are born, relatives and friends congratulate our parents, but while they are all happy and smiling, the baby is certain to cry. To those present, the baby's crying is a good sign, since it denotes healthy lungs. What they probably don't realize, however, is that the baby is crying with the soul's sense of relief at having met and overcome the many dangers that were present during conception and growth. Although at this stage we are relieved to have finally entered our incarnation, we are also anxious about the journey of life that lies before us. We are overwhelmed with an anxiety born of an instinctive realization of the many hardships that accompany an earthly life.

In every incarnation, we go through these fearful events not once but twice in our lives. Almost all of us cry when we are born and many of us also break down when our death is at hand. Those close to the dying person also shed tears because everyone feels sad when someone passes from life. In the process of birth, we travel down a dark path, the birth canal. The dying soul likewise travels down a road of fearful darkness as we pass on to the spirit world. So it is that our courage is doubly tested – at birth and at death. Why is this? It is to test whether we have the courage to step into a world of the unknown and start a new life all over again, completely from scratch.

LIFE IS LIKE A SCHOOL

During a lifetime here, we accumulate various valuable experiences, all of which are designed to refine the soul. Through them – through work, family, and all relationships – our souls can become more educated, elevated, and polished, before eventually returning to the spirit world. As a result, it is possible for us to transform ourselves into individuals of great character and significant depth. You will discover that everything positive and negative in your present life becomes meaningful when you realize that this is your whole reason for being here.

For instance, many of us born into the present era have experiences and occupations that did not even exist in our previous incarnations. When compared with people in previous eras, many people today also live a generally more convenient and comfortable life, as well as having the opportunity to travel and get to know and work with people from other countries. When we look at the world from a higher perspective, we realize that we are very fortunate to be born into this time, to be able to amass a great many experiences.

In most cases, the world will have gone through extreme changes since your previous life on Earth, and the differences will be staggering. Souls born today greet a much more technologically advanced era. People are able to travel vast distances by road and even fly to other countries. New experiences become possible and there are fascinating diversions, ever new ways to learn, and greater personal enjoyment. It is with this expectation of unique experiences that all souls hope to be born on Earth today.

Our new experiences on Earth can include trials, as well. Each and every one of us will experience problems, whether related to work, financial difficulties, illness, or a host of other problems. It is quite natural for us to wish we could escape such issues altogether. Your life might seem to be nothing but pain and doubt, and you might think to yourself: "I've had enough of this and I never want to experience it again." For example, anyone who has been sick for a prolonged period knows the longing for escape from the endless round of physical examinations, injections, and medicines. It is horrible to occupy a sickbed for days, months, or years and doubly frustrating when your body will not move or perform as it should. Some people are forced to spend years in a wheelchair or have mobility problems that require them to hobble about on crutches or with a cane.

Similarly, in your occupation, things will not always work out the way you wish. You might end up being dismissed from your job, perhaps as a result of situations that are completely beyond your control. Losing a regular income can cause difficulties at home, leading to everyone having to make sacrifices or to work harder to make ends meet.

Your guardian spirit and soul siblings are watching over you in suspense and anxiety. They continue to worry when you make mistakes in life, when you are sick or injured, or during the times you are having trouble in relationships. The experiences that life provides are still precious to accumulate, however, even though risks and dangers are part of the inevitable scenario. Even if the life ends relatively early, by way of a fatal illness or a tragic accident in childhood, the situations encountered and the lessons learned are vital to the overall experience of the soul.

Gender also provides important learning experiences. A given soul will not always be born as a man or a woman. Some souls are born in both genders in order to experience the differences at a material level. Only by so doing can a soul understand the problems and pains of each gender. Other souls may, however, incarnate in the same gender time and again to achieve the maximum experience of life as that gender. These souls choose to work in similar occupations repeatedly, in many incarnations, some of which would benefit from a specific gender. Ultimately, it is the need to grow and amass new experiences, to develop, and to gain a better understanding that motivates the gender and circumstances of a new incarnation.

When you consider such situations while asking the question "What is the purpose of my life here on Earth?" I hope you will begin to see that there is value that can be gained, even from difficult or traumatic situations. The simple truth is that human beings are born into this world, again and again, for the purpose of gaining experiences that are vital to the soul.

When you die, the life you just lived is preserved eternally in the memory of your soul. Without experiences gained as a human being living in this world, you cannot add to your soul's experience or enlightenment. When you come to fully appreciate the Truth, that you possess eternal life, it is possible to cope with whatever worries, trials, and tribulations that beset you in your current lifetime.

Over and over again – dozens, hundreds, or even more times – we go through the cycle of reincarnation. Along the way, we learn and accumulate diverse experiences. Every life is different and it needs to be because if a soul lived through exactly the same circumstances in successive lifetimes, that soul would not be able to amass the necessary experiences to grow and evolve.

FINDING THE TREASURE BURIED IN TRIALS

It is quite natural that people would want to avoid distress, suffering, and frustration in life. When we are faced with a hardship, we invariably wonder why we have to go through such a miserable experience. But when viewed from the other world, the situation appears quite different. In the other world, souls who insist on choosing a difficult life are respected as souls of the elite class. Souls about to embark on new incarnations actively plan to undergo many tribulations during their earthly incarnation, specifically so that they can strengthen and improve themselves through patience and achievement. When adults go to an amusement park, many of them find rides such as the roller coaster very scary. Many children, however, revel in daredevil rides. This is quite natural because they cannot have such experiences at home or at school. Only at the amusement park are such thrills to be found. This is similar to some souls choosing difficult and even frightening situations in order to experience the associated sensations for the purpose of improving the soul.

It would be hard, if not impossible, to plan a life that has no trauma or difficulties. Indeed such a life would be virtually useless for the growth of a soul. Few problems would mean few treasures. Anyone living a life with no hardship would be unable to gain the sort of wisdom that only comes from experiencing setbacks and difficulties.

Our souls go through many kinds of experiences in the course of many incarnations. They teach us important lessons from which we learn important things, but you may not be able to understand the cause of your problems simply by looking at the life you are currently living. In this life, for example, you might be the victim of a violent or fatal crime, or even become a criminal yourself. When you encounter this sort of hardship, it is invariably the accumulation of past lives that is significant. Only when you are once again in a position to look carefully at a number of lives will you come to understand that there is something vital you need to learn from your hardship experiences.

With each lifetime come various issues that you have to address and assess. Everyone is in possession of a "workbook of life" and this contains a number of themes for each individual. The workbook carries a list of experiences that the individual will encounter. These might be "involvement in crime at twenty-two years of age," "illness at forty-four years" or a host of other possibilities. We all have spiritual lessons we must learn. For example, if you were particularly bad at bringing up children in a specific incarnation, you might next choose a life without children to learn from the opposite experience and then be in a position to assess the learning across lifetimes.

In order to adopt the right attitude and see your life from this perspective, you need to accept the one essential Truth – that human beings have eternal life. Because each of us lives forever, we can be sure that death is not the end of our existence. Whether we are killed in an accident, die from illness, or pass away in extreme old age, our souls continue to exist.

Your Soul Is Who You Are

Some of this information may be strange to you and perhaps difficult to accept, but please believe me when I tell you that the body and the soul are not separate during an earthly incarnation. Rather, they represent one unit. This is a Buddhist perspective, which I often talk about. We might use the analogy of a car and its driver. The body represents the vehicle and the soul is the driver. A car moves because the driver operates the correct controls. The car is of no use without someone to steer it. Similarly, without the car, any potential driver becomes immobile. Likewise, to function in the world, you need both a body and a soul.

To achieve a higher happiness, you need to move forward one more step by realizing that your soul is your true self. To use another analogy, your body is like a suit of clothes you might wear. Death is like taking off your suit of clothes and reincarnation is like adopting a different outfit for your new life. Many people fall into the trap of believing that the soul and the body are two separate entities that are in constant conflict with one another. But the truth is that your true identity is the soul – your spiritual body – and your physical body is your removable outer garment. If you can raise your awareness to this level and maintain it, you will be able to experience great happiness.

While living an earthbound existence, we quite naturally see the world as our home. It is important to remember that this is not the case. The Real World is actually "the other world," your spiritual home where your soul siblings welcome you when an incarnation is over. Though you might enjoy the experience of occupying a human body for a while, your true home lies in the spirit world.

This might not be immediately obvious to you and you might well ask, "Then why do people grieve at the time of their death?" If we look again at the body as a suit of clothes, we can see that anyone might be sad when a much-loved jacket, sweater, or pair of slacks wear out and have to be discarded. We have relied on those clothes for a long while and are comfortable in them. But we soon accept that a new outfit is necessary and adapt to it. So it is with our bodies: We are accustomed to them, but they are of no use to us in our spirit home and so we must leave them behind.

We can carry this analogy further. If you were asked to choose between your life and your clothes, no matter how much you loved what you were wearing, you would always choose your life. In fact, under such circumstances, you would be quite happy to dispense with your clothes, even if they were designer-label originals. Clothes can be replaced but life is precious. The death of your physical body is just like throwing off your clothes in order to continue your eternal life.

When you think about passing from this world, try not to be too sad. Instead, think of death as going to a new place – or better still, returning home. The angels in the other world welcome the souls of deceased people, saying, "We appreciate your efforts. Working outside your true home must have been difficult. Welcome back." Your soul siblings will also be there to greet you. They know your life was difficult and they urge you to relax and make yourself comfortable.

It would be wonderful if you could begin to live your life from this new perspective. Death only means throwing off a physical body that may well have become weakened by sickness and age. It is not the end of "you" at all.

FINDING THE THEME OF YOUR LIFE

When you begin to accept the fact of eternity and the purpose of your time on Earth, your whole outlook will begin to change. Instead of shying away from various hardships and difficulties, you might even begin to enjoy them. This is how you might feel if you began to exercise more. When you first start to exercise, your muscles hurt terribly, but the more you work out, the more your body adjusts, and soon you can enjoy yourself.

With this new outlook comes the ability to adapt and to see things from a much higher perspective. Let us say that you have been going through great domestic and personal difficulties and you feel that your marriage is effectively worthless. With the new outlook, comes the ability to assess from an objective viewpoint and to change. Now you can see your relationship difficulties as a lesson from your workbook. And you can also contemplate the fact that your present troubles represent lessons carried over from a previous incarnation, which you now have the opportunity to get right.

All people have certain patterns of behavior and specific propensities in their personalities. When situations that are similar to past experiences reappear, people tend to behave in the same ways. It is similar to the different characteristics and special habits of vehicles such as airplanes, ships, cars, and trains. Much as each type of transportation has a unique mode of operation and steering, people have unique habits in the ways they deal with certain circumstances. It is quite possible that you have dealt with problems in different incarnations using a similar strategy each time, and a little contemplation will bring you to a realization of this fact. So, instead of leaving the same old issues to crop up time and again, it would be far better to look squarely at them now, during your present incarnation.

A clue to knowing what these issues might be comes from looking at your life here on Earth. Similar sorts of problems are not only carried across from one life to another, they also tend to predominate while you are here in your present life. Look at yourself and your life and see if this is the case. Each time you are confronted by some recurring problem, I ask you to analyze it, learn from it, and try to overcome what could be your weaknesses by seeing yourself objectively.

LIFE IS A SERIES OF LESSONS

Now that we know the purpose of living in this world is to gain new experiences and refine our souls, let's take a look at how we can apply this knowledge to our lives here in the material world.

There are two basic objectives in life. The first objective is self-discovery. The fact that you have been born with the unique character you possess is an indication that you must strive to discover the sort of life you should be living. By exploring yourself, you can eventually come to realize why you were born with your specific characteristics and talents and come to realize what sort of life you have adopted. Nobody can avoid this journey of self-exploration and self-discovery.

The second objective of life relates to the way you interact with others, that is, what sort of role you play in relationship to those close to you and in society as a whole. You need to look carefully and learn about yourself through your interactions with the world. If you lived entirely on your own, it would be difficult if not impossible to learn anything meaningful about yourself. Only when you are surrounded by all kinds of individuals, who have different ideas and alternative ways of thinking, including both those you like and those you dislike, are you able to learn anything relevant about yourself. With careful attention, you can learn from the different characteristics of individuals, work out whether your thinking is prejudiced or well adjusted, and become a more balanced person as a result.

Other people are not always likeable and don't always behave in a way that suits us, but the lessons they can teach us are still very important. Each of us should try our hardest to be thankful that we have this opportunity, because through such people, we are able to learn more deeply about ourselves as individuals. In the case of extreme individuals, it might even be difficult to believe that anyone with such opinions actually exists. You may sometimes be amazed at the range of thinking exhibited by your fellow human beings. But no matter how pleased, surprised, or even appalled you might be, it is essential that people with such a range of personalities should exist around you. They are the mirrors by which you gain a comprehensive view of yourself.

This is one of the reasons why we live in communities. If there were no one else around, we could learn absolutely nothing about ourselves. This is why God created the world. By bringing to birth a world in which human beings can refine themselves through their interactions with others, God deepens self-recognition and offers a range of possibilities to all of us.

THE WORLD THROUGH THE EYES OF GOD

As your spiritual and religious mind deepens and your abilities increase, you will eventually be faced with a curious fact. You will discover that you gradually begin to develop two perceptions regarding the world: the perception of distinctions and the perception of equality.

With spiritual refinement and experience comes the ability to perceive the differences between various individuals. Everyone is unique and carries individual qualities that are innate. Each of us manifests our true nature, our divine nature, and our abilities in different ways. You will find that it becomes increasingly easy for you to recognize the level others have reached on their own journey through life and how each person has unique accomplishments. This is what is known as the perception of distinctions.

At the same time, you will find that you also develop a perception of equality. Although there is such a variety of people, you will begin to notice that, despite the fact that people think and act in different ways, all living beings have equal value. With experience and meditation also comes the realization that all other forms of life, each plant and animal, possess a shining life force and that each entity, just like a human being, is undergoing its own spiritual development. This realization may come suddenly and it is indescribably mystical in its implications; you will begin to understand the thoughts and feelings of the animals and plants that surround you. Just like us, animals form families and struggle to find enough to eat. They also depend on each other, with some taking on demanding tasks while others adopt supportive roles. With experience will come understanding and you will eventually be able to recognize the equality that exists throughout all creation. This is what I call the perception of equality.

When you are able to grasp these two opposing views – the perception of distinctions and the perception of equality – you will also appreciate that they are integrated. To know this is to see reality through God's eyes. God always views things from both sides and with great compassion. Adopting this grand perspective, you will begin to appreciate the pain and suffering that exists in all life, yet you will also recognize the valiant effort all life-forms make to survive. From the smallest single-celled creature, all the way to advanced life-forms such as human beings, all have their pain and suffering to bear, yet all emit that essential spiritual light as they live together on Earth. This can seem very sad, yet at the same time it is immensely heartwarming. All seem burdened by suffering, but at the same time everything is bright and filled with hope.

Mastering these two opposing and yet reconciled views represents an essential step on the path to enlightenment. When you first begin, your perception of either distinctions or equality often becomes extremely sharp, but this is only half of your task. It is then necessary to go beyond it, integrate the two concepts, and hold both as equal and indivisible.

The process of unifying these apparently contradictory elements and gaining a multidimensional understanding of the world involves many of the necessary stages of enlightenment. In this, we find the reason why this world is not a world all on its own, but is, in fact, directly connected to another world, the Real World. The material world in which we live offers only a glimpse of reality. The path of spiritual evolution extends from this world into the Real World, from which everything originally came and to which it will all return.

Breaking through Your Limits

As I have said, it is inevitable that you will experience some degree of worry and pain during your life, but these difficulties are actually blessings in disguise. So, instead of fighting against sorrow and injustice, try to understand the value of the struggle and feel grateful for it. After all, if you had no worries at all, it would mean you had no opportunity for further progress on your spiritual journey.

Not all problems have solutions, but you need to treat even insoluble difficulties as opportunities that contain the possibility of infinite progress.

There is no need to lament the fact that your life has been filled with failure because failure always contains the seeds of the next creation, the germ of future growth. Transforming the way you see yourself — the progress and expansion that comes from self-recognition — is in itself development of your soul. It is to achieve this transformation that you were born into the world. In fact, achieving a transformation of your self-awareness indicates that you have gained enlightenment and achieved success for your soul.

I myself have experienced numerous transformations in the way I view myself. As I mentioned in the preface, back in 1985, I began to publish a series of books based on the spiritual messages I received from Divine Spirits in the other world. After publishing three books, I remember thinking that I had done enough, and that my mission had been fulfilled. I said to myself, "I have conveyed the Truth and that is enough to justify my present incarnation in this world." It seemed to me that, even were I to die at that time, I would have completed the work I was supposed to undertake. I had told people about the existence of the spirit world and the beings that live there. I had been able to publish the spiritual messages from the Divine Spirits and even from Jesus Christ. But I was mistaken that this was the end of my mission. At the time, I never dreamt that I would continue to be kept as busy as I have been, and yet I now know that I still haven't completed my task.

You might think that you have reached your limits, but you will soon find that new opportunities and necessary tasks present themselves. You might be absolutely certain that you have gone as far as is possible, that you cannot achieve any more, and that you are beset by the mistakes you made on the way. But usually, soon after having these thoughts, you will discover that you have surpassed what you thought were your ultimate achievements and gone beyond your former limits. When you come up against a brick wall in life, yes, you suffer, but you can also find ways to surmount it. Employ new ideas to overcome obstacles, and in so doing, you'll find a way forward.

So it was for me. It wasn't only after my first three books were published that I thought my work was finished. I feel exactly the same way every year. I reach a point at which I feel I have passed on everything that needs to be taught, and then, oddly, new themes present themselves. The reason for this is that the reactions of people who receive my teachings today are different from what they were in the past. And, in a changing world, I myself have been changing, and my audiences' invisible reactions are constantly encouraging changes within me.

As I approached my thirties, I was confident of my physical and intellectual abilities. I thought to myself, "I am strong, physically fit, and quick-witted. I know everything and can answer any question." As I grew older, however, I began to feel that there were indeed many things I did not know. I came across situations I did not understand and my confidence lessened as a result. The reason for this lies in the fact that in the beginning the people who gathered round me were interested primarily in spiritual matters. The knowledge I had was sufficient for me to answer their needs. As our organization received more recognition in society and the membership grew, all kinds of people became interested. People from abroad began to join in greater numbers. Many of these individuals read my teachings and heard my lectures and I had to respond to an ever-increasing variety of people. When I considered their reactions, I became more and more aware of all the things I did not know. The weight of my ignorance began to bear down on me and I felt distinctly uneasy.

Although I had been convinced I had sufficient knowledge and that the enlightenment I had achieved was adequate, and despite the fact that I felt strong physically and had sufficient willpower, as the years passed, I began to feel I was not equal to the task and my confidence took a knock. It was always when I felt that I had reached my limits, however, that I was able to develop to a higher level. Continued spiritual development is indeed a mysterious and wonderful process.

One of the processes of self-development at a spiritual level is that, in rising above ourselves, we sometimes begin to notice that others are failing in their own spiritual quests. We must take care to ensure that we are being truly objective in our assessment of those around us and it might sometimes seem that we are becoming overcritical. All the same, as our level of awareness rises, so does our ability to notice the mistakes and limitations of others.

This can also happen in the way we view ourselves. When we become aware of our faults and weaknesses, it is usually because we are about to undergo a transformation. It is actually very hard to recognize our own inadequacies unless we are on the verge of abandoning our old selves and about to move forward. People who remain satisfied with the way they are do not usually understand their failings. Even if they are aware of them, they try to keep them hidden from view, probably hoping that their good points will make up for their shortcomings. Those who believe they never make mistakes actually do so frequently but often remain ignorant of the fact. As your perception sharpens, you will increasingly be able to realize your mistakes before you actually make them.

You Can Change Your Fate

To understand and overcome your failings, it is very helpful to understand the tendencies of your soul, the patterns of your thoughts and behavior that determine the course of your life. If I were asked whether fate actually exists, I would reply that it does. When I suggest this, however, I am not saying that people live their lives according to a rigid script that leaves no room for improvisation and alteration. It is true that people have certain ways of behaving that are sometimes carried over between one life and the next. By looking at these carefully, it is possible to anticipate the direction life will take. It is only within this context that I suggest that fate is a reality. It is possible to anticipate what is likely to happen to an individual five, ten, or even twenty years or more ahead.

With practice, we can carry out the same procedure with regard to our own lives. I think it is necessary for all of us to look honestly at our good and bad points. When we become adept at doing so, it becomes possible to foretell, at least to a certain degree, where we are likely to succeed and when we will most probably fail. In this sense, there is such a thing as fate. All the same, this type of fate is possible to overcome. You can change circumstances through understanding the traits and tendencies of your own soul by carefully analyzing your strengths and weaknesses. This is achieved through a study of yourself and those around you. When you make your leap forward by sloughing off your old self, what fate had in store for you will change.

If it seems to you that your life is cursed and that your fate is so bad you want to escape from it at all costs, there is only one way out. You must gain a firm understanding of the motivations and tendencies of your own soul. Once you learn to do this, you will be able to foresee your future and understand what you must do to change things. And because you will be aware of some of the pitfalls ahead, it will be possible for you to take action to avoid them.

Look at yourself very carefully, watch your actions, and analyze your desires. Everything you need to know in order to educate your soul and find your path is present, even if it is not immediately apparent. You should strive to develop new strengths from your weaknesses. Meanwhile, you should also try to find the seeds of failure within what you consider to be your strengths. Once you manage to achieve a true and unbiased knowledge of yourself, of both your strengths and weaknesses and how they affect your future, you will be on the path to long-lasting success. So, although fate does exist, it is quite possible to discover it in advance and to improve it.

MODERATION IS THE KEY TO SUCCESS

There are also, however, forms of destiny about which you can do nothing. When these confront you, it may be necessary to resign yourself to them. A good percentage of the misery people experience in life is the result of excessive desire. Most people have a strong desire to grow. If this were not the case, there would be no progress or improvement in the world. It is fine to desire progress and improvement, but sometimes, people desire to achieve things that are beyond their capabilities. So, knowing and accepting your fate also involves understanding both your natural gifts and your limitations.

It is difficult for the Devil, even with all his tricks and guile, to bring down those who truly understand the extent of their abilities, strengths, and weak points. I would advise anyone to avoid being overconfident. Those who really understand themselves, warts and all, are very difficult to trap. Conversely, it is easy to trick and bring down those who have no knowledge of their limitations. All that is required is to lay a trap in their path and they will fall right into it. This often happens to people who believe they possess infinite ability.

In reality, human beings do possess infinite potential, but because they have certain weaknesses that appear repeatedly in their incarnations, until they resolve them, they face limitations. As I have explained, the way to overcome these is to look at your strengths and weaknesses, as well as those of the people around you, as you undertake a careful study of life. When you arrive at some obstacle that you are unable to overcome, simply think of it as a matter of controlling your desires. Moderation is the key. Startling success is not always valuable to your soul and might even bring you to ruin because it is probably safe to assume that a good half of the desires people experience are excessive and unnecessary.

Controlling your desires and being content with moderate and gradual progress means you will rarely experience major failure. Excessive desire is referred to as "attachment," and it is only by getting rid of attachments that ultimate happiness can be achieved. This is a path to happiness that is open to everyone.

It may sound strange, but it is a fact that in many cases people are happier if they never achieve what they desire. For example, many elected officials aspire to lead their countries one day, but in the majority of cases, it will turn out better for them if this never happens. Once a person has achieved the highest office, that politician is beset with comments about what he or she does and doesn't do; the leader is criticized for trifling matters and wonders why this should be. Imagine not being able to open a newspaper or turn on the television without hearing your name being ill-used and everything you do open to censure. Imagine not being able to walk out of your house unless you are surrounded on all sides by guards. In the end, what is seen as an unparalleled honor can lead to the greatest unhappiness.

The same can be said of everyone's desires. For example, people who are successful in their careers will probably have difficulty being the best husbands or wives. Some people feel unhappy because their children do not appear to be very bright, while other parents whose children are brilliant lose the ability to converse with them, leading to inadequacy and sadness.

SEEING YOURSELF THE WAY OTHER PEOPLE SEE YOU

We face limitations, but we have none. The causes of our limitations are found within us, but their boundaries are often set by other people's objective opinions. If you feel you are unable to get ahead in life, despite all your efforts up to now, you may need to look at yourself more objectively.

You may decide not to aim for material success. You could be content to work at a job that is not overly demanding but pleases you. If you are satisfied with such employment, you could go on to find meaning in life through other areas, such as religious activities. Should you decide, however, that you want to move forward and perhaps own a large business some day, you will not be satisfied with your present routine job. It is entirely up to you to choose the sort of life you will lead, but if you continue to feel that despite all your efforts you cannot move on to the next stage in life, it could be that you are not being realistic about elements of your own nature. This is when it is important to see yourself the way others see you.

To overcome difficulties and break through your limitations, you need to look at all problems from the other side, and see situations through the eyes of others. Whenever you feel you are not progressing, look hard for the reason and for the message the situation is seeking to impart. Your efforts will be rewarded and will allow you to discover the next step you should take in order to achieve further growth.

Life can be filled with various problems, but when

you realize and fully accept that life is eternal, you have received the greatest treasure imaginable. I would like you to remember that the hardship or distress you encounter on your road through life represents growth for your soul, and even if you struggle to solve a problem, you will be able to make it a great experience. It is my profound hope that you awaken to the true purpose and meaning of life, and that this knowledge will help you in the growth of your soul.

CHAPTER 3

The Spiritual Foundation
of Life

I N CHAPTER 2, WE discussed the eternity of the soul and
dealt with the meaning and purpose of our earthly lives.
In this chapter, I would like to explain why it is so vital for
everyone to accept and believe in the existence of the soul,
why we need to know the distinction between good and evil,
and why faith is so sacred. These represent three points of
reference that are vital to our education in spirituality.

The idea that human life is eternal is beyond most
people's comprehension. Although many people in the West,
partly due to upbringing, accept the concept of eternal life
and profess some sort of belief in an afterlife, they do so at
about the same level that a child comprehends a fairy tale.
Very few people have a solid understanding of immortality
and rely on it as a foundation for life. In a society that is
becoming ever more agnostic, those few who do fully accept
the concept are likely to be ridiculed or opposed by those
who follow an entirely materialistic doctrine.

People who find the whole concept of spirituality difficult to grasp may argue that, if God exists, why does God not help us to understand the Truth of life? Alternatively, they ask, why do we have to go through pain and suffering and make gargantuan efforts simply to understand the Truth? In the material world, we have ways to prevent people from becoming confused or suffering accidents. For example, we have pedestrian crossings at road intersections. The road is clearly marked and there are traffic lights that show red and green signals, telling us when it is safe to cross and when it is not. Would it not be sensible for God to offer us the same sort of certainty, so that people could more easily find their way? If God leaves us unable to understand the Truth, is it fair that we should have to face judgment after death? To some people, it seems unfair, irrational, and unscientific to face this ultimate judgment when they don't even know if there is an afterlife.

In reality, there are spiritual beings constantly trying to help us understand and make the right decisions. My past experience and the many messages I have received from the spirit world have taught me to have confidence in the fact that we are never alone. I understand, however, that most people remain unaware of being watched over by spiritual beings and this is how it should be. How very difficult it would be for the majority of people if they felt that they were being watched every moment and that their every move was subject to scrutiny. For many, that would be unbearable.

You have probably seen in television dramas a police interrogation room where people are taken when they are suspected of committing a crime. Typically, the only people present in the room are the interviewee and one or two police officers. But one wall of such a room is a two-way mirror, so that others can view the proceedings without being seen. This is a good analogy for the situation that exists between the material world in which we live our daily lives and the spirit world that lies beyond most people's comprehension.

Some might suggest that it is unreasonable and unfair that spirits in the other world can watch us freely while the majority of people cannot see them. Based on my own experience of the spirit world and the bearing it has on our everyday lives, however, I am sure it is better for most people not to see spirits or to hear their conversations. I know very well that it is sometimes extremely difficult to live a normal life while constantly interacting with spirits who exist in different dimensions. Too much awareness of their presence and hearing their voices all the time can interfere with every aspect of life.

The people who receive direct spiritual experiences from higher realms in Heaven, such as psychics, prophets, and religious leaders, are able to teach and spread the Truth about the spirit world to those who are busy living their everyday lives. Occasionally, other people who do not usually think about such matters also have spiritual experiences of their own. These experiences and explanations prevent people in the material sphere from completely losing touch with the Real World from which we all came and to which we will all return. Still, the vast majority of individuals are prevented from having direct spiritual experiences.

All of this protects people so that they can live a life of their own free will. Just imagine if you were about to choose your lunch at a local store and you were beset with a host of other customers, all advising you what to choose. It would become difficult to know what you wanted. Hearing voices from the other world or seeing spirits that live there would make it impossible for you to take the initiative or to exercise your free will. God created the structure and systems of the world in such a way that we can choose for ourselves and be responsible for the choices we make.

In many ways, life is like an obstacle course that has been specially designed for each individual to complete. Nobody will tell you how to climb this wall or to get across that stream. You are free to do as you like, and the way you complete the course will depend on the choices you make. Your performance will eventually be evaluated and judged, however, and you will be expected to account for your actions.

Each individual life on Earth is fairly short, especially when viewed from the perspective of the eternal flow of life through vast ages. Few people live beyond a hundred years, which is actually not very long and will be over before you know it. During the time you are here, you will go through all manner of experiences and struggle at points with pain and suffering. There are the four classic pains of birth, aging, illness, and death, as well as the suffering of separation from those you love and the trials that come with having to deal with people you hate. You will also suffer the pain of not getting what you want and the pain of physical desires taking control of your human body. The pains that arise from having a physical body lead, in turn, to a tendency to ignore the reality of the human soul. The mistaken belief that human beings are purely physical beings along with total dependence on the senses can lead you to the delusion that you can be truly happy simply by satisfying your physical desires.

To assist people in overcoming these pains and sufferings, religions teach that it is the soul and not the body that is the essence of self. There is nothing new about this teaching, which has been preached since ancient times and has been repeated to followers over and over, but many people remain unconvinced.

EDUCATION OF THE SOUL

It is in this context that I would like to talk about the education of the soul. In a world in which the majority of people are ignorant of the Truth, we need to provide fundamental teachings about the soul, life, and the world. In chapter 1, I introduced you to the term "teachers of souls." This is usually used to identify someone who not only provides us with useful knowledge but also has a pronounced influence on our character. Such a person helps us become better human beings. What I mean by "education of the soul," however, is beyond the level of moral education. It has a deeper meaning that includes in-depth education regarding all elements of life.

Education of the soul is education about the existence of the soul. Such teaching is based on the absolute understanding that the soul is the true nature of human beings. It also instructs us in how to educate, train, and transform the soul. The teaching of morals is essential, but recognition of the presence and importance of the soul is imperative and is something that is fundamentally lacking in the education system of most cultures at the present time.

To those studying religion or philosophy more than two thousand years ago, the reality of the soul was paramount, but as we get closer to the modern era, the concepts of spirit and soul tend to fade from view. In more recent times, the emphasis has moved to the functions of the brain and nervous system. What is more, ignorance about the soul and the more mechanistic way of viewing human beings is often considered a sign of academic development and progress.

In times past, the very heart of philosophy was to pursue essential questions such as: "What is the true nature of a human being?" "What is life?" and "What is the purpose of human life in the universe?" Philosophy united all fields of academic study, but soon there was such diversity that each subdivision began to specialize. Many experts emerged, each concentrating on one area of study, and the number of people who had a broader perspective decreased dramatically.

In modern times, the whole study of philosophy has become tremendously complex. It includes mathematical concepts and a deep study of logic. As a result, we can no longer purify the soul or attain enlightenment through studying philosophy. Philosophy has changed dramatically and has lost its original precepts, to its own detriment.

If we look far back in time at the works of Plato, it is clear from his writings that this early master of philosophy asserted the existence of the soul. Despite the fact that Plato is still studied and quoted, the vast majority of those who now read his ideas have not had the same spiritual experiences with which Plato himself would have been so familiar. As a result, modern "experts" on Plato rarely if ever touch on his concept of the soul. Beginning with Descartes and Kant, the tendency to separate the physical body from the soul has gradually grown stronger. In some ways, this might be considered a good thing because modern philosophers have helped to develop the academic world and brought specialization to their fields. But it is also true that philosophy has, to a great extent, lost sight of the true nature of human existence.

A similar state of affairs is evident in religion. In the past, the founders of religions were united in their understanding of the existence of the soul. But as hundreds or thousands of years passed, even people who had no personal spiritual experience became religious leaders. They learned their religion from books or established entire religious organizations simply to perform ritual ceremonies. In many cases, religion has forgotten about the soul and has become detached from its original, spiritual heart. In effect, religion has been turned into an academic discipline – something that exists in print and that one can read about. Along the way, it has lost much, if not all, of its substance.

Looking at these purely academic trends that have gradually invaded religion and philosophy, it is clear to me what those who reside in Heaven would think. They consider it essential that people on Earth should once again be taught about the reality of the soul. Without this knowledge of the soul and its immortality, people lose sight of the true nature and essence of life. They won't understand why they were born into the physical world

– to live, to experience, and eventually to die. Unless they know the true purpose of life, individuals will never be able to establish the right way of living. Without knowledge of the soul, no question about life or death will make any sense and no amount of observation of this material world will lead to real answers.

One philosophy that became very popular in the late nineteenth century and has influenced modern philosophy is existentialism. At its core lies the idea that humans are thrown into the world by chance, whether they like it or not. As a result, existentialism argues, people have no choice but to live blindly, as if groping about in the dark, uneasily and with no idea what to do. The influence of existentialism on modern philosophy can be seen in the latter's basic position that human beings have absolutely no idea who they are, why they are here, or what they are meant to study during their life on Earth. Thus, we are like children suddenly finding ourselves sitting at desks in the first grade of elementary school without any comprehension as to how we got there or what we are supposed to be doing.

I want to show you that this sort of philosophy is completely irrelevant to a true perspective of life, its purpose, and the mission that I teach. You are free to think as you wish and learn what you like. But there is only one Truth. Human beings are spiritual beings, and this fact cannot be both true and false.

What we really need to learn is that people are born into this world numerous times and that their various incarnations are for the purpose of training their souls through the cycle of reincarnation.

What I refer to as the soul is the spiritual being or energy that resides in the physical body. The body and soul in combination represent the complete human being. Often our spiritual energy extends slightly beyond our bodies, representing an aura, but generally speaking this energy adopts a human shape and fits neatly within the physical body. The spiritual energy that inhabits each one of us is what I refer to as the soul.

The crucial question is, of course, whether the soul really exists. If it does not, this means that only our physical bodies are alive. If it were not for the soul, human beings would be little more than machines. However, machines can only move and function because somebody is using them for a specific purpose and therefore directing their actions. Similarly, human beings have controllers that move their physical bodies about for a purpose. The soul is the controller. Without the soul to direct it, each human being would move about randomly.

Just ask yourself: "Am I living according to my own will? Don't I make choices and ultimately live the life I decide to live?" You can think for yourself, you decide what is good or evil, and you can also pursue freedom. You can seek, make the necessary decisions, and then live life accordingly, like choosing left or right, good or bad, right or wrong. This is why we are different from machines. It is of the utmost importance that we see beyond the physical and material parts of our lives and discover the true controller of the physical body – the soul. If you cannot do this, you are actually saying that you are nothing more than the functioning of your brain and nerves. Could this view ever have resulted in considering each one of our lives as precious? Could it ever have led us to uphold the dignity of each individual and could it ever have brought us to the concept of democracy or the overriding belief that every person is sacred?

Each person is sacred because God has given us life. The idea that all individuals count because of their God-given existence lies at the heart of democracy and fairness within society. Without such a foundation in belief, it might be possible for society to treat people equally, but they would then occupy a rank no better than physical bodies, like machines. Human beings are sacred because we all have a unique soul that can be improved and polished. The soul can become more brilliant as a result of effort and self-discipline. This is the true meaning of the sacredness of human beings.

Each of us has the ability to improve ourselves immeasurably as we strive to get closer to God. We all have the potential to grow through education, training, self-discipline, and enlightenment. This is the reason for human greatness. This is the dignity that God has given us and is the supreme privilege with which we were born.

The outcome of life will be different for each individual, however. Much depends on the environment in which we grow up, the education we receive, our experiences, and the level of enlightenment we attain. Thinking in terms of a number of incarnations, the progress of a particular soul depends on experiences encountered and lessons learned in a number of lives. In our present life, these represent hidden factors because we are usually not aware of their significance. They have a bearing on our spiritual maturity and the level of our enlightenment. Those who have incarnated many times and who have worked carefully through their workbooks on each occasion will be spiritually mature and will be able to see through to the core nature of experiences and grasp essential Truth easily. Those who lack this type of development will take time to reach a certain level of enlightenment. Nevertheless, every single person is equal and sacred in the sense that all are living under one law and the same principle.

What is this principle? It is the law that applies throughout the universe. It is a manifestation of the mind of God, God's thoughts, and the laws of divine nature. Every person has a divine nature, which means each person contains the possibility of eventually becoming one with God. If we live in accordance with God's laws, we can draw closer to God. Conversely, if we go against them, we are living our earthly lives in a way that is opposite to the Will of God and we become separated from God.

THE TRUE DISTINCTION BETWEEN GOOD AND EVIL

Since I had my awakening and began my spiritual quest, I have had many mystical experiences. What I have come to understand clearly during my years of passing on the Truth is the true nature of the distinction between good and evil. The two are often blurred in today's society and the difference between them is sometimes seen as ambiguous. In reality, there is a very tangible difference. Those people who live a life of goodness, who help others, and who have good thoughts pass through to the heavenly world. Those people who live in constant error, who never make any effort to improve, and who continue to perform evil deeds will not be able to return to the heavenly world. They either go to Hell or spend a great deal of time wandering in a realm close to this world because of their attachment to material pleasures and experiences.

I discovered that the soul is ultimately judged and found to be good or evil, without fail. This became one of the most important principles in walking my own path of enlightenment. Distinctions in the world are rarely so clear-cut. People in different groups hold many viewpoints about a host of matters. In democratic societies, it is the majority that wins. Different societies in different times throughout history have come to differing conclusions as to what is correct and incorrect, right and wrong. In spiritual matters, the situation is quite otherwise. From a spiritual perspective, the distinction between good and evil is not open to discussion and never varies.

A soul that achieves Heaven cannot be condemned to Hell the following day, nor can it travel back and forth between the two. The judgment on each soul is ultimately made without any doubt or confusion. People adhere to a multitude of religions, with different names for God, different rituals, and different teachings, but when it comes to what is good and what is evil, everyone is subject to an ultimate judgment, regardless of that individual's country, class, or religious affiliation. The sky and the sea appear to blend into one on the horizon, but in reality they are not at all the same. So it is with good and evil. No matter how things might look, good and evil can never mix; they are clear and distinct from each other.

The terrifying reality of life is that many people live for decades without knowing the difference between good and evil. This is like a small child tottering along the edge of a deep swimming pool. If the child leans to the right, he will be safe, but if he leans to the left, he will fall into the pool and be lost. It is therefore vital that we understand clearly the distinction between good and evil. This requires a firm understanding of the fundamental Truth: the soul is the essence of each human being, the soul is eternal, and the soul's existence encompasses past, present, and future.

We also need to understand that, depending on the results of our spiritual accomplishments and our life training in the world, we are ultimately divided into two groups: those who will achieve Heaven and those who are destined for Hell. There are two quite different destinies available to us. We must gain a clear understanding of what is right and what is wrong and know that the criteria for good and evil are based on the reality of Heaven and Hell.

The other world is largely separated into two worlds: Heaven and Hell. Heaven is a place of happiness and bliss, a Utopia where people who are filled with light and happiness live. People who live lives that generate lots of light, whose thoughts are filled with goodness, and who wish happiness for others return to this world. Conversely, people who live only for themselves and their personal desires and don't care whether they misuse, hurt, or even kill others end up in Hell.

If you say, "Okay, then all we have to do is return to Heaven," that is certainly true. However, the cause for the existence of Heaven and Hell is found on Earth. Heaven and Hell are created by the way people are living here, by their thoughts and actions. That is why Hell will not disappear until Earth becomes an ideal place. If we cannot accomplish this in the material world, we are only procrastinating and extending a necessary task into the next life.

To teach and establish the true criteria for good and evil, I have been passing on the opinions of angels, bodhisattvas,[1] and tathagatas[2] in Heaven to those on Earth. Like most people who choose a spiritual path, I have also had my own battles with Devils and malicious spirits. Gradually, I learned why these spirits became fallen souls and how it is possible for them to escape from their torment. Even the worst situations I encountered in my own life were not without purpose because recognizing the ultimate suffering of those who are cast down helped me to walk more confidently on the path of Truth. Based on these experiences, I have been able to teach others how they can protect themselves from being deluded by these evil spirits. My teachings have always been based on the Truth, backed by spiritual facts I have experienced. The human mind alone could never arrive at these divine conclusions, and the words of those who do not have a spiritual core cannot compare with Eternal Truth that comes directly from Heaven.

Spiritual beings known as Devils are mentioned in the writings of many religions, in particular Buddhism and Christianity. Devils are souls that are in opposition to the laws and principles of God. They are souls who do not feel ashamed

---

1   A bodhisattva (Sanskrit) is an angel of light who resides in the seventh dimension of the spirit world. A bodhisattva is motivated by compassion and is dedicated to enlightening and saving people through the Will of God. (Okawa, Ryuho. *The Science of Happiness*. Vermont: Destiny Books, 2009, p. 13.)

2   A tathagata (Sanskrit and Pali) is a Great Guiding Spirit of Light who resides in the eighth dimension of the spirit world. A tathagata is an embodiment of the Absolute Truth, a being who manifests love towards humans and instructs us. The term implies transcendence of the human condition. (Ibid.)

of wishing unhappiness for others; they are duplicitous and anxious to spread misunderstanding and darkness. Such entities appear in countless doctrines. As one example, evil or vengeful spirits are mentioned in Japanese Shintoism. They are described as beings who feel resentment towards people in the material world. They bear grudges, always seek revenge, and are happy to do harm to others. Whatever religion describes them, these Devils or vengeful entities representing the forces that are in direct opposition to the Will of God are active in the material world as well as in the spiritual realm.

When we stand on the edge of enlightenment, evil spirits of all kinds will rise to try and obstruct our forward progress. The reason for this is simple. It is very troublesome to tormented souls and malicious spirits when someone awakens to the Truth because once an individual has achieved enlightenment, he or she will be sure to pass on the Truth to others. Devils and evil spirits can only survive and flourish in darkness. The pure light from those awakened to the Truth reveals their tricks and schemes. You can be sure that if you walk the path of Truth and move towards enlightenment, a host of Demons and Devils will try to prevent you. They will tempt you with all manner of worldly pleasures and desires. Such Devils and evil spirits do exist in darkness. That is why we need the light of the Truth. When that light shines on the evil spirits, they fade and disappear.

We should never allow ourselves to be carried away or overly impressed by worldly success. No matter our status, education, reputation, income, or family background, our spiritual state will be judged as good or evil. Whether we are discovered to be good or bad depends on our state of mind, whoever and whatever we are. Even those of high rank or esteem in society, such as leading politicians, presidents of great international companies, and priests, ministers, or monks are subject to the same tests as the most humble individuals who have spent their lives in the slums. Those who are constantly under negative spiritual influences are abusive, and their hearts are filled with envy for others, anger, dissatisfaction, and complaints. These people will join the group of evil spirits when they leave this world. Then they will become active in trying to lead others astray, as surely as they were led astray themselves.

Because of the value placed on external achievements in the material world, it is easy to be lured into thinking that an institution or organization is wonderful simply because of the accolades it receives. A school, for example, can achieve the highest academic standards, but there is an enormous difference between a school that has religious Truth as its basis and one that does not. One high-ranking manager may recognize God's laws while his colleague at the same high level lives a totally worldly life. The difference between these two individuals, who at first sight seem to be doing the same job, is tremendous.

Those who have awakened to the Truth will gradually cease to see things from a worldly point of view because they will begin to recognize the real nature of others, regardless of background, income, or social status. They have had the strength to become independent of worldly values, or at the very least, not to allow themselves to be ruled by them. It is our duty not only to educate ourselves to the realities of Truth but also to raise our children with a constant awareness of the perspective and the thoughts of God.

LIVING WITH FAITH

When considering how to educate our souls and what the basis of this education should be, we must never lose sight of the fact that faith is sacred.

Not having a religious faith denies the existence of God. It is as if you are suggesting: "The world was not created by God and is not governed by God." It suggests that God has no power in the world, and that the world is a place of darkness. To such people, the world will seem dark indeed because as long as they hide under the roof of denial, the sun of God can never shine down upon them.

Who is most pleased to see people failing to find faith or losing it? It is the Devil. A total denial of faith in God will lead our world to be controlled by the Devil; it will become his world. A world in which faith is ridiculed and trodden on is a place run by the Devil. Having and maintaining true faith is the noblest characteristic of human beings. Like a wonderful flower, it should be nurtured and protected because it is the greatest accomplishment of the soul. We need first to understand fully the importance of faith and then to convey its value in all we do so that an ever-greater number of people have faith in God.

In these last pages, I have spoken about what I consider the true education of the soul. As I explained, it depends on recognizing that the soul is the real nature of a human being, that the soul lives eternally, and that the soul is polished through many incarnations of effort. Once you know that the soul is your true self, you need to awaken to faith.

Live your life knowing that faith is something sacred. Once you are shining brightly through practicing faith, allow that light to penetrate everything around you. Share it with as many people as you can and make your greatest effort to create a Utopia in our world.

CHAPTER 4

The Pursuit of Happiness

I N THE LAST CHAPTER, we dealt with the importance
of knowing the fundamental Truth and having faith. But
you might reasonably ask, "What is the substance of faith
and what virtues based on faith should I be practicing?"
Exploration of the Right Mind answers these questions. It
is based on the laws of the mind and the fourfold path to
happiness, which consists of practices that everyone can
apply to their lives. In Part 1, we focus on the laws of the
mind. Part 2 details the fourfold path to happiness.

PART 1

EXPLORATION OF THE RIGHT MIND

Goodness knows how many lectures I have given over the years,
but I have certainly offered many based on the universal laws,
hoping that those listening will, at some point in their lives, come
into direct contact with the Truth and awaken to it. I choose

themes likely to open their eyes to the Truth and lead them to walk a path to happiness. In particular, I nearly always focus on the laws of the mind at some point because these are the rules that determine whether people will ultimately be happy or unhappy. In this sense, they are of crucial importance.

One of the objectives of our organization is the scientific research of happiness, but what does this actually mean? It means studying and exploring the mind that invites happiness. In seeking to better understand the origins of happiness, the mind becomes the subject of our research, based on the assumption that each individual has a mind governed by certain universal laws.

How is it possible that we can all live under the same laws governing our minds when each and every one of us is a unique individual, with different backgrounds, personalities, and talents? The reason is that God exists. Because God exists, the minds of all people living apparently independently on Earth are subject to the same set of laws that respond to the reality and existence of God.

For many years, I have examined the state of mind that invites happiness or unhappiness and I have reached one fairly simple and convincing conclusion. This is best explained using an analogy. Imagine that the human mind is like a magnet and that it can attract iron filings or iron sand through its magnetic force. If the mind is in harmony with happiness, it will attract iron sands of happiness and the result will be many positive events. Moreover, I came to discover that just as a magnet attracts iron sand, so happiness is automatically drawn towards those who wish for the happiness of others.

If, on the other hand, we have negative thoughts, the mind has a negative force – in other words, a tendency to attract misfortune – and it will draw to itself iron sands of unhappiness. Negative situations will follow. There are no exceptions to this rule. Happiness will never come to those who consider only their own needs and seek their own enjoyment or success at the expense of others' happiness. The whole concept is very simple but also very true.

Some people might regard this as an irony in the world God created. They might argue that if we want water from a well, we simply throw down a bucket and pull it up. How can we quench our thirst by constantly giving away the water in the bucket to other people? Why should anyone be happiest when they concentrate only on the happiness of others? In saying that you should aim to make people around you happy, I do not suggest you have to sacrifice yourself and live a miserable life so that others can be content. What I would like you to know is that the very act of wishing others to be happy will ultimately bring you happiness too. People who concentrate exclusively on getting what they want from life are actually attracting the very opposite of what they want. Selfishness is not the true path to happiness and is simply a misunderstanding of the Truth.

RECEIVING GOD'S ENERGY

How on earth can wishing for the happiness of others have any bearing on your own state of mind? To explain this, I want to use another analogy of the nature of the universe. Although it may be invisible to you, the universe is filled with a positive spiritual energy. This unseen but very real energy is the power that brings about progress and that never stops providing people with joy and fulfillment. It is the power of creativity and love. Now imagine that this invisible energy is a liquid, like water, and that it flows throughout the entire universe via a vast system of pipes. One of these pipes travels directly to the heart of every individual and connects that person back to the source of the energy at the heart of the universe. Just as our homes are connected to a water supply, our hearts can enjoy an unlimited supply of the spiritual energy that is always available.

Much in the way we deal with water entering our homes, however, there is a method for utilizing the spiritual energy available to us. The life-giving liquid is of no use to any of us if we have no idea how to turn on the faucet so that it can begin flowing. Similarly, the endless flow of God's energy is always available to quench our spiritual needs and to bring us fulfillment, but it won't reach us at all unless we know how to access it.

Your ability to turn on the faucet to access the flow of energy coming from the heart of the universe, from God, depends on your state of mind. When you adopt a certain way of thinking, the faucet is turned off, but when you change your mind-set, it is turned on and the energy can flow indefinitely.

So, what sort of thinking ensures that your faucet to the power of God's love is turned on? If you are compassionate, kind, caring, and mindful of the happiness of those around you, you can receive God's energy through the pipes of the vast universe. If you try to turn on your faucet only for your own sake, the energy will eventually stop flowing.

Once you learn how to turn on your faucet in the direction of God, you need to show others how to turn on their faucets to receive the energy. If we all concentrated on making others happy, the energy of God's love and light would gush forth into creation like an inexhaustible well.

We can carry our analogy about the pipes connecting us to God's love a little further. In order to maintain an adequate home water supply, we have to ensure that the pipes do not become clogged. Obviously, water cannot run through blocked pipes. Why does a pipe clog? Generally, because of waste matter that gradually accumulates, restricting the flow of water until it eventually stops altogether. In the case of our spiritual pipes, the waste in the pipe represents the litter accumulated in the mind.

The blockage is often caused by desire. There is nothing wrong with desire itself. It is one of the driving forces required for life. Like everything else, desire was designed and given to us by God. Even the gifts God has given us can be misused. It is only when desire is used in the wrong way that it becomes a hindrance and a blockage. In particular, desire becomes a problem when it is used in a way that harms others. It clogs and blocks our direct communication with God to such an extent that the endless energy flowing in our direction eventually ceases reaching us.

Egotistical desires can distort and taint the pure energy coming from God. Even though the energy of the universe is essentially clear and pure, magnificent and beautiful, it can be contaminated in the process of flowing to this world, in the same way that accumulated waste in pipes gradually contaminates the water as it runs through them.

What I am trying to show you by using this example is actually very simple. Your ultimate happiness depends on the degree to which you attune the vibrations of your mind to those of God. Adopting the right frame of mind and acting in the correct way will ensure that your receiver is always attuned to God's transmitter. And what are the signals that are coming from God? They are love, wisdom, courage, justice, hope, joy, freedom, equality, fairness, progress, and a host of other vital gifts. All you have to do is to attune your mind to make the connection to God, and then you will be able to receive infinite energy of light.

THE ULTIMATE RIGHTNESS

There is a certain law that, if studied and applied correctly, enables you to receive God's energy and experience true happiness. This is a law I call Exploration of the Right Mind. In this context, the word "right" means a state of mind that is in accordance with the laws of the Primordial God who created the universe.

The rightness that I teach does not necessarily correspond to the results of scientific research or study. The rightness I talk about has its basis in the existence of God and the existence of the spirit world. What is right in the world of faith is eternal and immutable and quite different from what often turns out to be the temporary truths of everyday life and even of science.

Science, in the earthly sense of the word, can be useful to us. It is a yardstick by which we can make earthly judgments, but it cannot explain everything. Something that is considered right in a scientific sense is often a theory and has not been proven true. For example, science claims that humankind emerged several million years ago and that humans diverged from the chimpanzees four million years ago, but no one has presented concrete proof of this theory. Some schools teach this theory as fact.

To avoid unnecessary conflict, it is quite acceptable to follow the rules of society in particular settings, for example when we are at school. Just as Jesus Christ once looked at a coin bearing the image of the head of the Roman emperor Caesar and told his followers, "Render therefore unto Caesar the things that are Caesar's and unto God the things that are God's" (Matt. 22:21), there are certain things that are governed by the rules of the material world. There is little point in arguing with these because, in many respects, acceptance of them makes our lives run more smoothly. Even textbooks are not necessarily correct, however. They simply represent what is accepted as common knowledge at a particular point in time.

More than twenty-five hundred years ago, Shakyamuni Buddha renounced the world to become a monk, in order to discover the answer to why human beings have to go through the pains of birth, aging, illness, and death. But even today, two and a half millennia later, science is still unable to explain why people are born and the meaning of death, or prove the existence of the world after death. Buddha did have answers and what is more, answers that are still relevant. This is why, even in the age of science, religion remains vital. Even those who rely on the "rightness" of science, for example, doctors who treat us with medication or surgically remove tumors, should recognize the existence of the human soul and accept its importance.

The same is true in relation to legal matters. God did not create the constitution of any country; human beings did. The laws of any nation, even a democratic one, reflect only the opinions of politicians at a given point in time. Depending on the number of legislators belonging to a particular political party at a particular time, the legislation will differ. In this respect, it is easy to see that even laws made by humans are not always right. Politicians, judges, and lawyers may be experts in the law, but what they perceive to be right can be fundamentally different from what is right in the world of faith.

Perhaps you can now see why the scientific, medical, or educational definition of "rightness" is inadequate. You need not let this trouble you unduly. After all, we have to live our material life in a way that allows us to share definitions. What I ask of you is that you judge what is truly and inexorably right according to the criteria of faith.

The rightness I talk about does not work in the same way as, say, the answer to a mathematical problem, in which there can only be one correct answer. In the rightness of faith, there can be many right answers, dependent on the situation and the person concerned. The ultimate and irrefutable rightness is not something rigid or limited to one way of thinking. Even the Divine Spirits in Heaven have different opinions because they also have different personalities. These Divine Spirits present us with philosophies of a consistently high level, all of which are designed to lead people to happiness. There are, however, some variations in the way they perceive and approach the same issue.

It might be possible to assess whether a religious group is right or worth following by looking at its influence on society.

That so many religious groups exist and that they present different ways of thinking merely indicate that there are wide variations in people's needs. This should not be overlooked. In the same way that what ultimately brings the greatest happiness can vary from person to person, the specifics of what is considered right may vary. Still, religious diversity is aimed in one direction, towards the Will of God. This is the true meaning of rightness, so Exploring the Right Mind is to seek a rightness or the state of mind that accords with the Will of God.

PART 2

THE FOURFOLD PATH TO HAPPINESS

You may wonder, "How do I explore the Right Mind?" The answer to this question is "by practicing the Principles of Happiness." If you focus on exploring them and do your best to put them into practice on a daily basis, they will assure you a happy and bright life. There are four Principles of Happiness: the Principle of Love, the Principle of Wisdom, the Principle of Self-Reflection, and the Principle of Progress. These four together constitute what I call the modern Fourfold Path. These principles are not independent of each other; rather, they are closely related. Each principle contains aspects of the other principles. Following each of them carefully means you will always be able to walk the path of happiness and ensures that you will be able to return to the heavenly world after death. You will be able to improve yourself to become an Angel of Light.

If you make efforts to explore the Right Mind and keep the Principles of Happiness at the forefront of your mind while you study the Truth, practice self-reflection and prayer, convey the Truth to others, and make a contribution as a member of society, you will continue to make spiritual progress. The four Principles of Happiness constitute the daily practice that leads to spiritual refinement. Let's take a closer look at these principles.

THE FIRST PATH — THE PRINCIPLE OF LOVE

Left to their own devices, many human beings tend to live for themselves; in other words, they are most likely to take from others. Just like animals they feel they want to get more and more. But I want you to remember that as human beings we are special; we are the children of God. As such, we have to suppress some of our less admirable desires, and instead, to cultivate love for others. We have to be kind to those around us and try to live a life that is of benefit to them and to society as a whole. This is the meaning of giving love to others.

When you awaken to "love that gives," you raise your state of mind to a higher level. You achieve a higher level of enlightenment. Most important of all, once you awaken to the importance of "love that gives," your mind is no longer attuned to Hell.

GIVING LOVE TO OTHERS

When people think of the word "love," in most cases their minds turn to the sort of love that exists between a man and a woman who are attracted to one another, or the love that exists between parents and children. Most individuals have a strong desire to receive love, and if they don't get enough of it, they suffer. Think about it carefully because, if this is the way your mind works, you need to alter your way of thinking. You need to stop considering only what you can get from others. If everyone only took love from others, this would inevitably lead to a worldwide shortage of love. What is required is that we all become net suppliers of love. If we do, the whole world will be filled with love.

A society with insufficient love, or one that is entirely materialistic and based on "love that takes," is like a huge hospital filled with patients who are constantly crying, "It hurts everywhere. Give me more medicine. Do something to ease my pain." On the other hand, if there is love to spare, more people will be happy and healthy from a spiritual point of view.

This is why you should try to do what you can to give love to others. Try doing things that benefit those around you. Before demanding happiness for yourself, try bringing happiness to others. Moreover, if you give love, you will discover that any pain inside you is automatically eased and your worries begin to disappear.

TAKING LOVE FROM OTHERS

A great percentage of our pain in life comes from attachment. Attachment is the pain of not being able to make others do what we want them to do. In Buddhism, it is known as the pain of not getting what we want. In his teaching on pain, Shakyamuni Buddha taught that there are things in the world we can never have, no matter how much we want them. The pain of being unable to get what we want is merely another manifestation of not being loved by others or not being appreciated. When we feel we are not being appreciated, whether emotionally or materialistically, we suffer. Materialistic appreciation can include food, clothes, income, a car, a house, or almost anything we crave in this world. Emotional appreciation can be expressed by kind words, thoughts, and actions, or by others' respect for our social position. Generally speaking, appreciation is not something we can achieve for ourselves; rather, it is something we get from other people. If we focus too much on receiving appreciation from others, the result is pain.

An analysis of the suffering people face in the modern world reveals that it often comes down to individuals feeling they are not being given enough by other people. You may feel frustrated at not being able to achieve a particular aim in life; you might think that your salary is too low, despite being good at your job; it could be that you think your partner or friends do not sufficiently appreciate you. Myriad situations can contribute to our anxiety and even mental pain, simply because we cannot get what we most want.

Materialistic issues are bad enough, though we can often resign ourselves to these, but if our worries are emotional in nature, especially matters associated with personal relationships, it is difficult to put the pain to one side and to carry on as normal. No matter how hard we try, we cannot force other people to change the way they think. It might be that the person from whom we crave attention and recognition seldom acknowledges us, or that those we love the most show us little affection. Meanwhile, we get plenty of attention from people we have no desire to impress and those for whom we feel little or no affection. This is the way of the world – things often refuse to turn out quite the way we wish they would.

Problems experienced in childhood can sometimes lie at the heart of dissatisfaction later in life. Once children have grown up, they may continue to feel their current suffering had its roots in the way they were treated or the lives they were forced to live as children. They may feel that their parents were too poor and so they as children lacked many of the material things that other children took for granted. It could be that, because of their parents' status, they were unable to receive the sort of education that would have been of more use to them, and they might, consciously or subconsciously, blame their parents for not being able to give them the upbringing they craved. This is especially true in modern society, where family breakdown is common and divorce affects many families. Those brought up in a divided household might think that this has contributed to their own, later relationship difficulties or their lack of confidence.

Unfortunately, we cannot turn back the hands of time. Many people would like a chance to relive their lives. This includes parents perhaps regretting aspects of the way they brought up their children. Even if our parents recognize they might have done better by us in some way, however, there is nothing they can do to alter what happened years ago.

Our anxieties and heart-felt complaints about the past can resurface many times in our adulthood. We may expect our boss or our partner to give us the recognition or affection we failed to get from our parents decades before. Unfortunately, in most cases this doesn't happen and we end up feeling the same sort of dissatisfaction with these people that we felt with our parents.

The desire for social recognition generally represents a desire for paternal acknowledgment. People who feel that their fathers did not give them sufficient recognition seek compensation from an authority figure for the lack of acknowledgment. We cannot always receive the preferential treatment we might feel we deserve. A boss, for example, has a responsibility to look after many people and try to act fairly towards all, not showing favoritism to anyone in particular. If a company executive displays personal likes and dislikes towards particular staff members, it affects the motivation of the whole office, so executives make every effort to avoid doing this. Thus, we are unlikely to be singled out for special treatment and get compensated for the feeling of dissatisfaction we had towards our fathers.

Dissatisfaction with your relationship partner may have its roots in the belief that you did not receive sufficient love from your mother. If you feel you do not get the recognition or affection you deserve from your partner, it is possible this too relates to childhood. Perhaps at some level, you think you did not get the attention or love you deserved from your mother. It could be that your mother was extremely busy simply trying to earn a living. Perhaps you have brothers or sisters and so your mother's time had to be divided among all her children as equally as she could manage. Those who did not receive sufficient love from their mothers in childhood often find themselves attracted to someone who is the opposite of their ideal, and fall for a harsh, sharp-tongued partner, the type who will only hurt them more. As a result, they end up repeating the experiences they had as children.

Wounds to the heart suffered during childhood come to the surface in different ways in adulthood and many people end up living unhappy lives as a result. Years can be spent searching for people and situations to compensate for feelings of unhappiness and dissatisfaction – someone or something to fill the emptiness. Those who lead their lives in this way can become like a bottomless pit; no matter how much they are given, they always demand more. Eventually, there is no end to the demands and those around them grow tired of the situation and stop giving altogether. The result is greater unhappiness and dissatisfaction.

People with a tendency to take endlessly often remain totally oblivious to what they already have or what blessings come their way on a daily basis. They focus instead on what they cannot have. These people remain dissatisfied no matter how completely others devote themselves to fulfilling their demands. They fail to see how much their partners are actually doing and opt for being critical about what they feel is lacking. A particular woman may, for example, complain to her partner that he always gets home late from work, failing to recognize that success in business often demands long hours. But if the same partner returned home early every day, at the sacrifice of a decent salary, she might then criticize him for not working hard enough.

If we spend time looking closely at ourselves, we should recognize that we are far from perfect. Given that we have our own imperfections, is it right or proper that we should demand absolute perfection from everyone else? The fact is that none of us is perfect. Those who expect perfection in their partners or think that they will never be satisfied until they meet the perfect partner need to realize that they have turned their back on happiness forever. Those who pick on a single fault in others are looking for a reason to be unhappy.

Once you start down the road to constant taking, there is no end to the journey. Be it in a material sense, such as objects and money, a physical sense, such as health, or the intangibles, such as social reputation or fame, you will never be satisfied. It will be quite impossible for you ever to say, "This is the best; this is perfect!"

In most cases, you create your own suffering. So, if you recognize that you have a tendency to take constantly from others, now is the time for you to start to change your way of thinking. Believing that you can be happy by getting everything you want is a cruel delusion. Be happy about what you have already been given and look to the strengths of others. Instead of thinking always about the 10 percent that is lacking in others, thank them for the 90 percent they have given. Don't concentrate on what those around you do badly; instead, acknowledge others' good points. If you manage to achieve this, you will be amazed at the way your view of the world will change. Changing your evaluation of those around you is, in reality, a first act of giving to others.

If you want to achieve real, lasting peace and contentment, you need to abandon the idea that you can only achieve happiness by receiving from others. So, right now, at this very moment, stop taking from others. Look carefully at what you have been given and work out how you can give something in return. Even a small effort in this direction will ultimately make a great difference. Don't expect any reward, because that is just another form of taking. Be content to give, and in the end, you will be satisfied with the result.

TURNING YOUR PERSPECTIVE TO GIVING

You can never achieve true and long-lasting happiness as long as you are constantly craving what you do not have. You have already been given a great deal, so start by offering thanks for what you have. You will then start to feel the need to offer something in return and begin to live a life of giving. The truth is that there is no way to be unhappy in a life that involves "giving back." Almost the moment you start to offer something to others, you will begin to feel happier yourself.

It is a little like a mathematical equation. If you give back 1 percent of what you have been given, you will achieve 1 percent happiness. If you give back 10 percent, then you will achieve 10 percent happiness; 50 percent will bring 50 percent, and so on. When you turn your perspective around and begin loving others and giving to others, unhappiness disappears from your life and you start to create happiness immediately.

There is nobody in this world as happy as those who consider the happiness of others to be their own happiness. People who find pleasure in seeing a smile on the face of another because of something they have been able to do for that person develop a mentality that cannot avoid happiness.

When you start thinking about what you can do for others, your mind will start to work in a different way. Let us look again at the example of feeling like you are not getting enough attention or recognition from your boss. With the new mind-set, ask yourself, "But what have I actually, tangibly done for my boss?" Now that your perspective is changed, the answer will likely be: "I have actually done very little." You may realize that, although you thought you were doing your best, others thought you only worked hard to get something out of it for yourself. You could discover that you felt as though no one acknowledged your contribution simply because you didn't know how others perceived you. In this situation, as in all others, you need to put yourself in others' shoes, think how they might perceive you, and do what you can to be supportive of them. In other words, think about their happiness. Repent the fact that you failed to do so before and do what you can for them. This is your own path to happiness.

There will always be people around who insist on having their own way and who take every opportunity to draw attention to themselves, but nobody ever manages to achieve true success in this way. Although such individuals might seem to be getting on well for a while, they fall down eventually. Such people often achieve a position that is beyond their capabilities. They appear confident and they seem to be getting on in life, but an upset is almost certain to happen. For your part, try to be modest. It costs nothing to act with humility. If you are always courteous to others, no matter who they are, while making constant effort, you will not fail.

People might remember an insult for years, but they also remember a compliment. It takes only a moment to be pleasant, but it has a profound effect on the person concerned. Here is some good news. Improving your relationships is free; it costs not one single cent. All you need to do is change your way of thinking and offer a few kind words. In so doing, you also guide others onto the path that leads to happiness. There may be a small effort involved at first, but when you see the results, it no longer feels like an effort.

So, if you are suffering at this very moment, if your life is filled with pain, instead of looking inwards, look out. See how many ways you can think of to give love to others. As soon as you do this, your own worries and pain will begin to diminish. It might sound simple, but these are small steps towards an enlightenment that will open your eyes.

When you begin to practice love, you have already begun your own journey to happiness. There will be greater enjoyment in every day, and you will become more and more delighted by the happiness you are able to bring to those around you. Start with what you can do for others. If you find joy and happiness in seeing others smile, you have already taken the first step towards Heaven. People of this sort go to Heaven when they die.

Conversely, there are people who feel envy and jealousy, and they are far from experiencing true happiness. Those who are jealous of others think only of their own happiness, and their hearts are in darkness. The prerequisite for entering Heaven is to find joy in seeing happiness reflected in another person's eyes. If you have mastered the Principle of Love, which is the first step in walking the path to happiness, this alone is enough to open the gate to Heaven for you. Although this principle may seem simple, it is critically important and really quite profound.

THE STAGES OF LOVE

The development of love involves four stages: fundamental love, nurturing love, forgiving love, and love incarnate. The first stage, fundamental love, can also be called neighborly love. It is the love you have for those you come into contact with on a daily basis, such as family and friends. It might seem to be a fairly low level of love, but this is not the case. If you master fundamental love, you will be able to enter Heaven. So, this is a very important teaching. What is more, it is the first step towards achieving enlightenment. Your start must always be to practice fundamental love.

Once you have mastered fundamental love, and you have fitted yourself to enter Heaven, you should then look at nurturing love, which is a higher level of love. In order to practice nurturing love, it is sometimes necessary to be strict with others. Nurturing love is the love expressed by a teacher or leader. It requires wisdom. As an example, schoolteachers cannot express their love in a classroom situation by spoiling their students or allowing them to slack off in their studies. Like anyone else, students are happy to receive praise but will generally work harder for a firm teacher. Compliments and kindness alone are not sufficient where the education of others is concerned. You have to teach them that, to open up a positive path to the future, they have to try harder, even if they experience some hardship along the way. Practicing nurturing love requires wisdom, along with a combination of kindness and authority. If you manage to achieve this level of love, you will be recognized as an excellent leader in the world.

Higher than this, and the next stage in development, is forgiving love. This is a spiritual state that embodies even deeper love than the first two stages. As long as you are conscious of the self and your own ego, while keeping yourself separate from others, nurturing love will be the most elevated stage of love you can reach. When you achieve a higher spiritual state, however, your perception of self begins to change. You realize that, although on one level you are yourself, at another level you are not. When you devote yourself totally to your mission, it eventually occurs to you that you are not a separate entity at all and that you have been specifically chosen to carry out a mission for God. You come to feel like a component of the Almighty, as if you are a "finger of God." You finally realize that your very presence in this world represents a part of God's Will.

As you develop this profound perspective on life, you will be able to view things with a great sense of compassion, and you will be touched by the fact that all living things undergo spiritual refinement in this world. No matter how degraded or evil a person may be, you will be able to perceive the light of goodness shining within that individual – his or her divine nature. At this stage, it will become abundantly clear to you that the suffering you see in even the most reprehensible people is entirely due to wrong ways of thinking and mistakes in their hearts. You will understand that wrong thinking was what led them to do wrong in the first place. When you attain this state of mind, you will discover within yourself a deep compassion, even for those who have committed crimes. It will be instinctive for you to help them to learn a better way and to polish their own divine natures. You will love them for their divine nature, the essence of God within them, even if others find it difficult to hold such people in any regard.

You will achieve a level at which it is possible to be moved by all living things in the world. Your appreciation for the life of plants and flowers will grow and you will see the divine light shining in animals. They too are striving to live their lives to the fullest and undergoing a spiritual refinement of their souls. They use the wisdom they possess to find food, they struggle to protect themselves from predators, and do all they can to raise their young successfully.

You will ultimately realize that animals have essentially the same nature as human beings, even though they may be a long way from actually being born as human beings in the cycles of reincarnation. Animals have the same basic feelings of joy and anger, sadness and pleasure as we do. And though you may not be able to see it yet, animals all seek to be human one day, through a long, long process of reincarnation. When you attain the level of enlightenment that allows you to see the divine light in all living things, you have entered the world of forgiving love. Things that were not apparent when you were in the stage of nurturing love will be self-evident and you will become forgiving.

The fourth stage of love, love incarnate, is the love of the tathagatas. This is a sublime state, about which you need not concern yourself. Concentrate on practicing fundamental love, nurturing love, and forgiving love. Love incarnate is a spiritual state in which your very existence represents the spirit of the age that shines light on the world. This is not something you seek, but rather something the world and later generations will acknowledge. Nevertheless, you can aim to be like the sun, bestowing life on all beings. You can wish to embody compassion, like a cloud that blesses nature with rain, quenching the parched earth with the benevolence of water. This represents a wish to manifest love incarnate. It is a desire to cast light not only on the people in your immediate vicinity but also on those all over the world.

In comparison to the grand scale of love incarnate, the love you manage to offer to family and friends may appear insignificant. Loving those you contact on a daily basis might not seem like much against an Earth full of need, but this is your first step on the road to developing greater compassion.

What I have itemized here are the different stages of love, but these stages often overlap each other. Each stage contains within it elements of the others. Fundamental love contains within it elements of nurturing love, and nurturing love has elements of both fundamental love and forgiving love. Everyone can even practice a degree of love incarnate. We can start within a family. A father can shine as a father, a mother as a mother, and the children can shine as children. Whether at home, at work, at school, or in the community, all of you can create love incarnate on a small but important scale. What makes each stage different from the other is which aspect of love is being expressed most strongly. The love we express appears at different levels at various stages in our development. In fact, the different stages of love correlate with the levels of enlightenment.

It is important to realize that we need to stop seeking love from others and instead concentrate on giving love. This is a profound blessing because it means you will be able to enter

Heaven if you can manage to follow the teaching. It may be impossible for you to practice giving love if you lack wisdom, however. In your desire to express your love, you might sometimes spoil others or inadvertently praise someone who is doing wrong. If you find yourself in such a situation, you need to call on your wisdom. This means there are times you must be stern with people, even against your will. It is part of guiding others, like a mother or father disciplining their children. This is a form of nurturing love you must also master.

As you develop nurturing love, you will soon be able to differentiate between what is good and what is evil. It isn't necessarily God's Will that you focus too strongly on distinguishing between the two. Forgiving love transcends this distinction. In other words, when you develop a deep compassion for all living things, you will be able to rise above good and evil.

Try to be like a bright torch in the darkness and shine at your most brilliant throughout your life so that you can give light to as many people as possible. Strive to be like a lighthouse in a harbor so that you can shine your light as far as possible. This is the wish to practice love incarnate. All seekers of the Truth must learn these developmental stages of love and engrave them into the core of their souls.

Most likely, you will stumble at first. Even when you do your best to show love to everyone, you will still quarrel sometimes with your partner, your children, your friends, or people out in the wider world. At no time will you be able to say, "I have finished with this stage of development and so now my spiritual education is complete." There are always going to be times when you have to return to the starting point. It is important to check yourself and your actions constantly in order to continue with your spiritual education and refinement.

This is the Principle of Love. If everyone understood this teaching, the world would be a peaceful place. These lessons add a new perspective to the Christian teachings of love. Although Christianity has always preached love, there are still countless conflicts in the world. If what Christianity has to say about love is transformed into a doctrine of compassion, by adding Buddhist teachings on love, all conflict will inevitably end. Thus, spreading these teachings on love throughout the world would bring happiness to humanity.

THE SECOND PATH — THE PRINCIPLE OF WISDOM

The second Principle of Happiness is the Principle of Wisdom, which is about knowing important spiritual facts and fully understanding the Universal Truth. Truth is not obtainable from worldly information. This is because the Truth comes directly from God. You can, however, get nourishment for your mind and your heart by studying books written about the Truth or by listening to lectures on the Truth. Even through the written or spoken word, you can feel the existence and presence of God.

When people who have been living a cold life, a life of pain and suffering, are enlightened to the Truth and awaken to faith through prayer, self-reflection, or study of the Truth, they feel energy flowing into their chests, warming their whole bodies, and even bringing color to their cheeks. This is the light of God and it comes directly from the Angels of Light in Heaven.

Everyone has the chance to experience this. When you feel the warm light filling your entire body, you are standing at the door that allows you to communicate with your guardian and guiding spirits. To stand at this entrance, you need to know the Truth, dispel your delusions, and let the scales of ignorance fall from your eyes. Knowledge is power, and by knowing the Truth, you can change your life. This is the Principle of Wisdom.

LACKING IN INTELLIGENCE

Earlier, I pointed out that there are many people who remain unhappy because in their estimation they do not get the love they feel they deserve from others. I explained that for these people the path to happiness lies in the Principle of Love, which states that you can find happiness by giving love to others. In this section, I would like to look at another group of people, those who experience suffering and pain because they bemoan their lack of intelligence.

This is something suffered by countless millions of people, though, strangely, most think this issue is unique to themselves. In reality, 99.99 percent of the population worry that they lack intelligence, but because people cannot look into each other's minds, they feel they are alone in this concern.

Let us take academic background as an example. You may wish to be like people who seem filled with intelligence and who graduated from the top universities. But if you imagine that these people believe themselves to be intelligent, you are probably mistaken. Actually, people who do well in education are more likely to suffer from an inferiority complex. Those who do not study but spend their time enjoying themselves are far less likely to share this sense of inferiority. It is the people who have devoted themselves more or less wholly to study who suffer the most when they find themselves behind others. For such high achievers, even one mark in an examination seems to mean the difference between genius and mediocrity and it can cause them despairing anguish. None of us is immune to doubts about our own intelligence when we measure intelligence solely on external criteria such as academic achievement.

What about those people who have graduated from a top-ranked school and who have an excellent academic record? If they are asked if they are happy, the answer will not necessarily be yes. Such people have their own issues that trouble them. For instance, they may distress themselves by thinking, "I did well in my education, so why can't I be materially successful in the world?" They may worry that they don't receive the accolades they expect from others or that they cannot make more money.

This is a universal problem. Actually, it is often the case that the better you are at academic studies, the less you earn. People who do exceptionally well at school may stay in the academic world and become teachers, lecturers, or professors. On the other hand, those who studied less but who were good at enjoying themselves and traveled, took temporary jobs, and became experienced in the ways of the world are likely to be successful when they do get a full-time job. They can make swift progress and earn higher salaries. Although they may not have worked as hard as they could at school, they make greater efforts in the workplace and succeed as a result.

People who have spent long years studying may also suffer because they cannot understand how it is that their classmates who spent their time playing and having fun manage to be so prosperous once they start working. The truth is that experience of life is itself a good teacher and the things that can be learned by living a full life are not covered by any university lecture.

Today, only few stand at the top of the academic system, and if judged on exam results alone, the overwhelming majority of people seem to be academic failures rather than successes. If happiness or unhappiness depended on academic records alone, it would mean that the majority of people were unhappy. It is not true that those who lack academic ability always fail while those who are good at study always succeed.

Of course, good academic records or high scores can lead to success if you continue to make further efforts based on what you have achieved. But if you just sit back, simply remain content with your results, that will be the end of your progress and you will not accomplish much. Those who were successful in school could very well face difficulties later on. Those who work hard and make the effort achieve success eventually. For this reason, it is important not to regard academic records or qualifications as being absolute.

Everyone is given an equal supply of talent, although it may be in different areas. Some are good at studying, others at something else. If you feel you are lacking in one area, you will find that you are gifted in some other field. You may not yet know where your talents lay, but you should know that everyone has talents. Knowing this will probably bring comfort to those who did not do well at school or did not get into top universities.

MAKING SPIRITUAL PROGRESS

You probably think that intelligence is something with which certain people are born. You may bemoan your lack of innate ability or regret that you could not achieve higher academic results in your first twenty years of life. It is true that some differences in intelligence are evident, even in small babies. The same is true when children are assessed by tests in elementary and middle school. As a result, it would be untrue to say that heredity has nothing at all to do with intelligence. But don't be fooled by such statistics. At the time you die and your life is assessed in the spirit world, you will receive a score that is based on what you did *after* you were born. Heredity has nothing whatsoever to do with our spiritual life score. We all, no matter what our background or circumstances, have it within us to make spiritual progress and being born with a silver spoon in our mouths will not save us from the inevitable judgment.

Each person starts at a different point, but evaluation after death is based on each individual's progress, regardless of where that person began the race in terms of intelligence or social standing. After we are born and begin to grow, effort is required of all of us to make progress in life. The amount of effort each person makes is evaluated based on the law of cause and effect. The more effort we make, the more we will be able to achieve. It is important to look at life from this perspective.

The material world is a competitive place, and to be quite frank, there are more losers than winners. No matter what start you had in life, if you allow yourself to be labeled a loser rather than a winner and do nothing about it, your whole life could be miserable and unhappy. If you are the sort of person who worries about your innate abilities, just remember that, in the final reckoning, what really matters is the amount you were able to grow. It is your rate of development and the degree to which you exerted yourself that count. The circumstances that prevailed when you were born, even your past lives, have nothing to do with the overall progress of your present life. You will only be assessed in terms of what you do *now*, in your present lifetime. This is something I would like you to remember.

Another point to remember is that genius cannot compete with effort. People who genuinely make an effort can never be beaten. Even those who are labeled as extremely bright will become as dull as ditchwater if they fail to apply themselves, even for a relatively short time. Although it is sometimes difficult to improve, it is very easy to fall back. This has nothing to do with inherent intelligence or fate. Even children born into the most privileged households, who are surrounded by every opportunity and who go to top schools, can go astray. They can become delinquent and a constant cause of worry to their families. This is not the result of fate or even an issue of intelligence. It is about what they value, their way of thinking, and how they perceive the world.

In any case, intelligence in an academic context, or even a genetic one, is not the same as intelligence gained from real life. Experience brings an understanding of the laws of success, which are not taught at school. Academic studies may give you a strong platform on which to build, but you can only learn the laws of success as a result of your own experience.

As long as we make comparisons between ourselves and others, we will not ultimately be winners in life. Rather than making what are usually pointless comparisons, look at your own life. Examine the progress you have made since you were born and strive to make more.

The ultimate battle is the one you fight with yourself, and everyone has the chance to win a stunning victory. Even those who never seem to put a foot wrong and score success after success may come to a point where they fall because they felt that they lost a battle against others. It doesn't matter how far they have come, they can be beset by misery and depression. Some of them cannot bear the pain of not being promoted when colleagues are. They think they become losers in life when they lose in competition with others. Their definition of success or failure is judged solely on the speed of promotion or who gets ahead of the competition.

We must all learn that progress in our lives is relative. In other words, the only person with whom you are competing is you. So, although it may be true that heredity has a bearing on intelligence, it is not the most important factor in life. Concentrate instead on looking at your spiritual score you have managed to achieve as a result of your own efforts and find happiness in that. If you are able to feel joy at discovering how clever you have become, there is no failure or defeat in your life.

THE POWER OF KNOWLEDGE

Generally speaking, you are more likely to succeed in life if you concentrate on what you understand the best. Success is more difficult to achieve if you are always approaching situations in which you have little or no experience. For example, if you know how the pieces move in a game of chess, you can easily win against someone who does not know the moves. If you pit yourself against a chess master, however, it is extremely unlikely that you will win, unless you too are a master. This is because the chess master has spent a great part of his or her life learning strategies and closures. You can't hope to compete unless you have the same knowledge. Life is much like a game of chess: The more knowledge you have, the less likely you are to lose.

When faced with the unknown, your ratio of success will rarely better 50 percent and there is no way of telling whether you will succeed or not. But if you are facing something in which you already have significant experience, your potential success rate will rise to near 100 percent. It is easier to win anything once you know the ground rules and how to proceed.

When it comes to the experiences of life and especially its challenges, most people are amateurs. Few devote themselves to a study of the challenges they face. For this reason, they are almost certainly doomed to failure. To avoid failure, we all need to gain knowledge first. You might ask how to go about this. There are, in reality, many ways. You can read, which is very important. You can get information from watching television, learn from movies, and listen to talks given by others. Whatever method you choose to use, when you encounter things you do not understand, you need to find the relevant information and material on which to base your decisions. If you are truly conversant with the subject because you have taken the time and trouble necessary to understand it, failure is much less likely.

Experience of life can also be a great teacher. Without a good experience of life, failure is always a possibility. As noted earlier, not all knowledge emanates from a classroom. Those who have lived closeted lives, no matter how well educated they may be, can't have a great deal of knowledge about the way the world works. They have no knowledge that there are people in the world who will do all they can to bring about their failure, and traps await them if they are unwary. They probably do not understand the dangers that face them because school may not have taught them about the existence of suffering, setbacks, and delusions in the world.

A few people are lucky enough to find a route to success without ever having to face setbacks but most, at some stage, will experience them. If you are aware of the pitfalls in advance, you are at a considerable advantage. It is important to be aware how specific people will react in a particular set of circumstances so you can react accordingly and appropriately.

Good bankers know all too well what will happen if they lend money to a certain type of person. They have a wealth of experience available to judge whether the potential loan will be a secure one or a disaster. If the bank manager is able to grasp what any situation entails, this will avert an unnecessary mistake and secure the bank's assets.

You have to learn about every aspect of life, and that includes evil. Even if your every intention is geared towards the good of the world, you will still have to encounter its evil at some stage. Know your enemy, because this is a big part of dealing with evil.

There are people in this world whose every intention is to cheat and trap others. Even if it is not actually intentional, some individuals will resort to this sort of behavior when they find themselves in certain situations. To prevent them from wrongdoing is also a form of goodness you can practice. By allowing evil to spread, even good people become the accomplices of evil. Therefore, you need to broaden your range of interests and carefully study the sources of evil in life, as well as the origins of corruption, failure, and setbacks. By doing so, you can prevent problems before they even occur, avoid failure yourself, and live a life of happiness.

There are limits to what anybody can experience, but if you watch your friends, parents, siblings, relatives, and friends diligently, you can still learn a lot. Look closely at why people fail, what leads them down a path of wrong, and what makes them go astray. There is no lack of examples if you keep your eyes open.

Those who have sufficient time to spend complaining about their own ignorance should spend that time in study. As a result, they will gain more knowledge and will be able to make correct decisions. This is a way to walk the path to happiness.

TURNING KNOWLEDGE INTO WISDOM

Today, we live in an information age and we are provided with the best circumstances to learn. So many books are published and so many educational materials are available that the human intellect has reached new heights. Never in our entire history has the world seen so much mass intellectualism as exists right now. Compared to those who lived in times past, people today possess an almost god-like knowledge, or at the very least, have the opportunity to access it.

Given that we live in such a privileged era, it would be wonderful if everyone alive today would make a thorough study of the Truth. This is why I am presenting the Principle of Wisdom here. Naturally, this principle begins with study of the Truth, but that does not simply mean *storing* the knowledge. I would like you to put the knowledge into practice in your daily life and in your efforts to help others also to reach the Truth.

Remember your workbook of life? When solving the problems in your workbook of life, you will exhibit certain tendencies in the areas in which you have particular difficulty. You may have specific problems in relationships or issues in some other area of your life. A good and coherent knowledge of the Truth will act as a sound basis for solving your problems, and it is important to put the knowledge you gain into practice. Then you are able to say, "I see how this should be done. This is how I can free myself from worries, solve my problems, correct my shortcomings, and achieve liberation." There is no end to the small discoveries you can make on a daily basis as you walk on the path to enlightenment. When you can utilize your knowledge and experience it as part of your enlightenment, you can convert your knowledge into wisdom.

In this way, build a basic knowledge of the Truth through study, make use of it in your daily life, and convert this knowledge into wisdom. You will then be able to use this wisdom to guide others. For example, you may have gone through an unpleasant divorce or been dismissed from your work. When you meet people who are suffering the same sort of problems and you have mastered those experiences through your understanding of the Truth, you will be able to offer them sound advice, together with words of enlightenment, that will open their eyes and help them overcome their difficulties. You may even be in a position to rescue someone from deep depression or even potential suicide. You need more than just knowledge about this world to save such people. You cannot save them unless you have studied the Truth and have gained an understanding of the Truth of the spirit world and the true essence of life.

So, no matter how much you may have suffered in the past, once you gain knowledge of the Truth, you will be able to turn your former problems into experience. In turn, the experience will allow you to speak words of wisdom to guide others. It is for the sake of the help you can offer to the world that you need to turn knowledge into wisdom.

Universal Truth for the Twenty-first Century

Numerous religions and philosophies are of ancient origin, and some remain locked in the past. I believe that if something is going to be relevant to our lives today, it has to reflect the circumstances and values of the present and the future. It is important that we remain open to new knowledge. We should be quite prepared to adopt new concepts or technology as long as the concepts or technology have the capacity to bring people happiness.

Of course, there are certain fundamental laws that have not changed for thousands of years and these are impossible to distort. But the world is subject to change and never more so than in the present era. If we forget this, what we learn will be irrelevant to everyday life, and modern minds will not understand or accept the Truth we teach.

Doubtless, if we were living in the Stone Age, we would worry our heads about how to make a better clay pot, but Stone-Age wisdom is no longer adequate to support complex needs in the modern era. The timeless Truths that have been around since the days of Buddha or Jesus, however, can wear the clothes that are provided by scientific breakthroughs and information technology to help people solve their problems in today's world. What I offer to you is the timeless Truth that can meet the needs of modern society, based on progress and a recognition that society and the world constantly change.

There are always going to be situations that lie outside of our field of expertise, but we should remain open and willing to absorb new knowledge. All kinds of information are available to us, including input from the academic world and the media and we at Happy Science embrace it all. Unlike some religious organizations that tend to remain closed to innovation or advancement, we remain open and happy to learn. This is because we have confidence that the message we carry is timeless. It also demonstrates that we have the flexibility to change if we find mistakes in ourselves.

THE THIRD PATH —
THE PRINCIPLE OF SELF-REFLECTION

The next stage on our path to happiness is the Principle of Self-Reflection. Once you know and understand the Universal Truth, you will never be able to live the same way as you did previously. You will likely realize that you have made many mistakes in your life – in your thoughts, actions, or words towards others. This is not unusual because people cannot live their lives without ever taking a wrong step.

You might think that once an event has taken place, it is fixed forever in reality and cannot be altered. In a material sense, this is true. If you drop a vase, it may well break and then all the glue in the world won't make it look exactly the way it was before; nothing will make it perfect again. In the same way, you might think that having done things you now regret, you will never be in a position to put these situations right.

You have now been offered the light of salvation, however, and that light is self-reflection. If you regret something you did in the past, if you truly repent and reflect deeply on your actions, the sin will be wiped from your past. This is because what happens in the mind encompasses past, present, and future, and so the mistakes in your mind can be undone. This is why we are given a chance to practice self-reflection. If it were impossible to undo mistakes, there would be no point in self-reflection.

What is more, your contemplation and understanding of where you went wrong offers far more than simple forgiveness. When you practice genuine self-reflection, you will receive support, encouragement, power, and energy. This comes to you directly from Heaven, and it supports and nourishes you through life. Therefore self-reflection does not simply turn a minus score into a zero. The blessings you receive for awakening to the Truth will far outweigh what you had before, and your life will be happier as a result.

In effect, you will be reborn. When you awaken to faith and practice self-reflection, you get the chance at a second life – a new birth that takes place while you are still living in the world. No matter what sort of an individual you were before and no matter what kind of life you were living, if you continue to practice deep and sincere self-reflection, never stop loving others, and keep searching for the Truth, you will become a different person and your life will be irrevocably transformed. It is our passion at Happy Science to spread the word about this Truth, and to become living proof, exemplary role models, of the transformative power it has on people's lives.

THE POWER OF SELF-REFLECTION

The material world in which we live and the spirit world exist side by side. In the spirit world, self-reflection works according to the same principles as the laws of physics. Whether or not you practice self-reflection in the material world determines your destination in the spirit world after death.

When souls live in the material world, to a certain extent they are blind. They make mistakes through ignorance because there is much they do not know or understand. God and the angels know this and they have tremendous compassion for those who make mistakes while living earthly incarnations. Even angels would not be able to avoid making mistakes if they were born into a physical world and lived the sort of lives we live now.

Of course we make mistakes. In fact, we have been blessed with the freedom to do so. Human beings are free to make mistakes because they also have the ability to correct them. Although a broken vase can never be fully restored, the human heart can be. The heart will be whole again in a spiritual sense, and in fact, will be more splendid than before.

Your mind contains an area called a "thought tape." This is where all your thoughts and actions are recorded. Everything you have ever done since the moment you were born is recorded here. Negative thoughts and actions are recorded in red as losses. You can look at all of these entries in the light of Truth and repent your wrongdoings. The act of realizing that you went wrong and should have acted or reacted differently sets you free from guilt or pain, as long as you are determined never to plant these seeds of negativity in the future. Once this has been achieved, items that were written in red turn to glorious gold.

It doesn't matter how bad you might think you have been during your life. If you reflect on your past with a pure heart, you can erase all the red entries as surely as if you had a magic eraser. This is a great power that God has given us. It means that right now you can make a new start. You can change yourself and you begin by practicing self-reflection. When you have achieved a certain level of self-reflection, your past sins will be entirely erased.

I once gave a lecture entitled "The Enemy Within," in which I told the story of Angulimala, an infamous bandit who lived in India at the time of Shakyamuni Buddha. About a mile from the ruins of the Jetavana Monastery, the ancient Buddhist center in India, there is a large burial mound beneath which lies Angulimala. It is much larger than any of the other burial mounds in the area and even larger than those of any of the ten disciples of Shakyamuni Buddha. In fact, it is the largest tomb close to the Jetavana Monastery.

Angulimala was a terrifying criminal who is said to have killed a hundred and perhaps even as many as a thousand people. One day, however, he saw the error of his ways. He repented deeply for his past actions and joined Shakyamuni's order. He underwent daily spiritual discipline with his begging bowl, while the local people pelted him with stones. In this way, Angulimala repented constantly and profoundly and strove hard to discipline himself in order to become an Angel of Light. People were eventually so touched by his tremendous efforts that they built a great tomb for him after he died. Those who created Angulimala's tomb recognized that the effort of a conversion from evil to good has a tremendous power of salvation. Even today, twenty-five hundred years later, people still come to pay their respects to him.

A pure person who lives properly and correctly, without a single blemish of evil, may have great power to save others, but those who have committed numerous crimes, then genuinely repented, devoted themselves to goodness, and started their lives anew also have the power to save countless souls. Buddhism recognizes this fact. Instead of preaching that sinners and even murderous criminals put themselves beyond redemption, it suggests that someone who turns over a new leaf and embarks on the path to enlightenment can gain greater power than someone who has never committed a single sin. Such people have the chance to develop an even stronger light to guide others. This is the power of self-reflection that I want you to know and understand. And of course, there is also the right prayer that comes after practicing self-reflection. You can use the power of right prayer to create a better future.

FIGHTING SPIRITUAL DISTURBANCES

One of the factors that cause people to stop short of success, and instead, walk a path of failure is spiritual disturbances, or the influence of stray spirits and evil spirits. People who did not believe in the existence of Heaven or Hell while they were alive or those who followed a misguided religion, may find it impossible to return to Heaven after death. These restless spirits will most likely go to Hell, but they generally try to remain in the material world in one way or another. Basically, they do not want to die yet.

There are only two ways in which stray spirits of this sort can remain in the world. One is by possessing another person and the other is by haunting a particular location. Because these spirits have such a strong attachment to our three-dimensional, material world, they cannot leave it behind. Those who find themselves possessed by such spirits may notice their life taking a turn for the worse. You should not be overly frightened by talk of evil spirits, curses, and the like, but it is a fact that spiritual disturbances are real issues in life.

It is impossible to be precise, since there are no actual statistics, but it would not be far from the truth to suggest that more than half the people living in modern society are on the receiving end of negative spiritual influences at some time and to some degree. In some cases, individuals can be influenced by more than one spirit.

If a person who is possessed becomes like the spirit possessing him or her – that is, they share the same values, an identical outlook on life, and the same behavior patterns – it becomes difficult to suggest who is actually in control. It is not uncommon for a possessed individual to develop the same habits as the dead person, and in the end, even take the same road to ruin. It can be disconcerting to watch this happen.

When a person destroys him- or herself in a particular way that results in death, sometimes another family member will make exactly the same kind of mistake. This has nothing to do with fate or destiny. If you have the same tendencies as your departed relative whom you suspect has not returned to the spirit world in a positive way but has remained within you, it will be necessary to make the effort to correct your negative tendencies.

How do people change when they begin to come under negative spiritual influences? The most obvious sign is a tendency towards massive mood swings, in particular becoming quick to anger and to fly into rages. When people are possessed, their worldview changes dramatically and they begin to see many situations from an opposite standpoint. Earlier I discussed the shift from taking love to giving love; the last thing possessed people want to do is give.

Those who have come under a negative spiritual influence generally feel terrible. They suffer from a persecution complex and are forever complaining about other people, the circumstances of their life, the bad luck they face, or their environment. Possessed people are quick to criticize those who are happy or doing well, but they continue to do nothing to help themselves or others. They only notice the bad points of those around them and believe everyone is their enemy. Then they gradually begin to feel that they are no longer themselves, that they are controlled by something outside of them. They find that their life swings from one extreme to the other. If they begin to suffer from a lack of sleep or develop the habit of drinking to excess or taking drugs, they may eventually become incapable of detaching themselves from these kinds of spiritual influences.

One of the ways to avoid falling under negative spiritual influences is to maintain a reasoned, rational approach. It is very important to maintain a logical mind. When you are spiritually affected in a negative way, you can take some initial, concrete steps. For starters, you should ensure that you get sufficient sleep, try to look after your health, and do your best to stay in good physical condition.

Although it is essential to stay healthy physically, there are other weapons you can employ when struggling against negative spiritual influences. The simplest one is self-reflection. If you have fallen under a negative spiritual influence, you should not entirely blame the spirit who is affecting you. Those who have been possessed for some time undoubtedly have tendencies and quirks that attune them to a particular malevolent spirit. In this sense, you are not fighting with the spirit possessing you, but rather, you are engaged in a battle with the evil within. If you find that you are surrounded by evil attacking you, it is because there is something inside you that attracts it.

With self-reflection, you will be able to address the negative tendencies in your mind. Once you do so, no malevolent spirit will be able to find a home within you and will soon detach itself. If you feel that your mind is attuned to Hell and you are under negative spiritual influences, start with what you can do yourself. In this situation, self-reflection will serve as your weapon.

LETTING GO OF YOUR ATTACHMENTS

Buddhism teaches us to get rid of our attachments because attachment is the main reason we are affected by negative spiritual influences. The root of attachments is the material world, and such attachments are often the source of our distress. In many cases, this worry and anxiety is what is transmitted to evil spirits.

If you know where your attachment lies, the way out is simple. If, on the other hand, you do not recognize what your attachments may be, ask yourself what it is you think about most commonly throughout the day, at the times you are relaxed and not concentrating on anything in particular. If there is one thing to which your mind constantly returns, that you mull over time and time again, this could be the sort of attachment you need to address.

You may have an attachment to something that happened in the past, for example, a bad memory from childhood, an ex-girlfriend or ex-boyfriend, or some sort of confrontation that has taken place in your life, possibly at work. You may be thinking about your personal responsibilities all the time or about some specific issues. If you realize that you have been concentrating on the same thing, not on just a single day but perpetually, this is your attachment. There are times, however, when attachments help you achieve a particular goal. If you suspect that this is the case, you need to be certain that you are directed towards an ideal and not just something that becomes a source of pain. Evil spirits plug themselves into people by way of these attachments. Without a doubt, that is how they sneak in. This is precisely why you must rid yourself of your attachments.

So, how do you go about eradicating attachments? As I mentioned earlier, one method is to alter your attitude from one of taking to one of giving. Another method is to shift your way of thinking to something else. For example, if you think of nothing but your intelligence, possibly because you suffer from a deep inferiority complex, rather than spending your time worrying, you should use it to study.

Alternatively, you could tell yourself, "All things are transient. All material things belong to the material world, which I will eventually leave behind me. In the final reckoning, the only thing that really matters is the victory of the soul." This is a way to rid yourself of your attachments. Remember that defeat in this world is not a defeat in life – the real life of your soul. It doesn't matter one jot what other people say or how you are evaluated in this world. The opinions of the material world have nothing to do with the final victory you seek. When you keep your mind focused on the real battle, victory for your soul, you will be able to eradicate your attachments, and once your attachments are cast aside, you can also get rid of stray malicious spirits.

If you are dealing with something you are unable to change through your own efforts, be indifferent to it and let it pass you by, without ever losing control of your mind. Live with a pure heart and go forward without attachments, like the flowing of a stream. Try not to dwell too much on the past. What has happened has happened and cannot be altered. The future *can* be changed, however, and you can make a great effort to do this. You may continue to regret what happened in the past, but once you have repented your misdeeds, do not focus too much on what cannot be altered by repentance. Live your life to the fullest and look for the lessons from your experiences that will help improve your life in future incarnations.

Even though you succeed in removing a possessing spirit, if you continue to hold on to the same worries, the spirit will find its way back. Once you have cast off the spirit possessing you, it is important to strive to retain a positive outlook on life. You have to make an effort not to let your personal vibrations resonate with those of evil spirits. So, once you have rid yourself of them through self-reflection, lead a positive and constructive life to ensure that your wavelength is never again attractive to these malicious visitors.

In this section, I have discussed the Principle of Self-Reflection. You need to be responsible for any spiritual disturbances that affect you and to take initiative in freeing yourself from them. Self-reflection is the simplest weapon to fight against negative spiritual influences. Looking carefully at yourself is a component of the path to enlightenment and a way to achieve happiness. The starting point of this path is always you.

THE FOURTH PATH — THE PRINCIPLE OF PROGRESS

The fourth Principle of Happiness is the Principle of Progress. This can be explained in many ways, depending on an individual's spiritual stage of development. And because each person's situation is different, it is somewhat difficult to apply the same explanation in all cases.

You need first to look closely at your own mind and contemplate the concepts of love, wisdom, and self-reflection that I have already explained. What you achieve from these principles will be realized as the Principle of Progress.

Through mastering the Principles of Love, Wisdom, and Self-Reflection in the correct way, the Principle of Progress will also flow in the right direction. In relation to the Principle of Love, it will be in the direction of loving others. If you are only concerned with receiving love and constantly exercise your willpower in that direction, however, both you and those around you will become unhappy. When practicing the Principle of Wisdom the right way, wisdom will contribute to your progress and the world, but if your thoughts are aimed in the wrong direction, you will be unhappy. You can use self-reflection to correct any mistakes or errors you make on the way. It is very important to be unselfish and check your thoughts and actions because those who are unrepentant will direct their thoughts in a negative direction. When you study, analyze, and find the answers to each of your problems through self-reflection, you will be able to enter the path of progress and direct your thoughts in a positive direction. And if by mastering love, wisdom, and self-reflection, you reach the Principle of Progress, you are on the right path.

THE POWER OF THOUGHTS

This principle is essentially based on the knowledge that humans are spiritual beings and that the spirit world is a place of thought, a place in which thoughts become reality. Those who embrace hellish thoughts will gather in large numbers in the other world and as a result, create a genuine Hell. In the realm of Hell, the spirits make each other suffer in an existence of distress and pain. Meanwhile, the spirits in the heavenly realms all support each other. The spirit world is a realm where thoughts are actualized. It is, in effect, the Real World. Thoughts are the true essence of human beings, and the body is simply a vehicle, or a means, of manifesting these thoughts. It is important to start thinking this way.

In our world of matter, it takes a certain amount of time for thoughts to become reality. We also have to use various tools or objects to actualize our thoughts. For example, it takes a certain period of time for us to travel from one place to another by car or train. But in the spirit world, things are very different. There, if we wanted to travel from one place to another, we would only have to think of the destination and we would be there. Everything in the spirit realm is instantaneous. As the Chinese Buddhist philosopher T'ien-t'ai Chih-i (538–597) observed, "One thought leads to three thousand worlds." Time and distance do not exist in Heaven or Hell, a reflection that is profound and even frightening.

When you are thinking about the spirit world, direct your interests towards the higher realms. Divine Spirits may be able to visit you, or they might offer you helpful inspirations. If you show too much interest in the spirits that inhabit Hell and attune yourself to them, however, they will grasp you and stay with you, which is very uncomfortable. It is important to avoid an interest in these spirits.

Thoughts are extremely powerful. In our world of matter, although certain things can obstruct the realization of our thoughts and they are not always manifested in a straightforward way, thoughts are always realized in the long run. Our thoughts gradually solidify like a flow of lava becoming rock. There may be slight differences in how much or how our thoughts are manifested, but both good and bad thoughts lead to results. This is because we take steps every day to actualize our wishes. Although the manifestation of our thoughts might not always be obvious, the manifestation is an undeniable fact.

The fact that our thoughts produce outcomes associates our world with Heaven and Hell. For instance, someone who has a strong wish to murder another individual is creating a very negative and hellish thought. That person may end up killing the person in question, to the great detriment of his or her own soul, or the person may eventually be murdered him- or herself. Negative thoughts always lead to negative outcomes and create their own Hell. If everyone wished others only misery, the world would turn into Hell. If, on the other hand, everyone maintained a wish to make others happy, Heaven would be established here on Earth. Our material world can turn into a Heaven or a Hell, depending on the kind of thoughts we have.

This is the basis of the Principle of Progress and what you need to understand. The law of thought is that both good and bad thoughts will someday be manifested. Bad thoughts attract negativity, while good thoughts attract goodness. This is a law of the spirit world and it always works this way. In order to deal with this fact, you need to gain an understanding of good and evil thoughts, and then to realize that your thoughts have the ability to make concrete changes in the world.

The Desire to Create Happiness

I would like you to believe that your thoughts will always be realized. It may take, ten, twenty, or thirty years, but they will always come to fruition in the end. Even if you fail to live long enough to see the results on Earth, you will be able to see them from the spirit world.

As an example, we can look at the life of Jesus Christ. Some people suggest that his role was intended to be that of the savior of humanity, but that he was crucified and died before he could achieve his objective. People who look at the situation in this way might suggest that his mission was not fulfilled. After all, even his twelve most loyal disciples denied him and fled. Although Jesus died on a rough wooden cross, his wish to save humankind has come about since his death. You can see from this that thoughts sometimes seem not to have been manifested in the short term, but with the passing of time they come to fruition.

The tragic events of Jesus' life influenced the course of Christian history for the next two thousand years. Although Christianity is in essence a good religion, the apocalyptic aspect, born of Jesus' end, remains strong among Christians, and this has led to further tragedies over the years. Since thoughts always become realities at some stage, we all need to be aware of and careful about what sort of thoughts we have in our minds. It is necessary to assess what could happen as a result of a thought in the future. What, for example, would be the result if a major movement were created as a result of your actions based on any particular thought?

If your own happiness is of the sort that will benefit the world and if it is your wish to extend genuine happiness to everyone, your thoughts are right and will cause no problems, either now or in the future. Your personal happiness and the happiness of humankind should be realized as one. We need to combine our thoughts and work together towards the happiness of all humanity. I would like you to make it your goal to contribute to the happiness of the whole and to build a personal happiness to achieve this end.

There are people who care only about achieving their own ambitions and are willing to resort to wrongdoing as a result. Even if people appear to be successful in our world, without the Right Mind they may commit evil deeds. If their ultimate goal is simply to achieve personal wealth, they may well be involved in crimes to realize their wish.

When it comes to your own plans and ambitions, you need to check carefully to ensure that achievement of your goal will contribute to the happiness of all humankind. If your thoughts are aimed in the right direction, support others, and are intended to fund a reservoir of happiness for all your fellow human beings, whatever you are hoping for will definitely be realized, through your continuous effort across a period of time. Your enthusiasm, your effort, and the length of time you work on it are the factors determining the extent to which your wish is realized. This is one of the laws of achieving progress.

It is my profound hope that those of you who study the Truth are successful in your lives because the more successful you are, the greater will be your influence for good. At the same time, it is important for all seekers of the Truth to realize that you should never become a slave to money, absorbed in gaining promotions, or conversely, increase your attachment by remaining stuck in the same position.

It is my earnest desire that the happiness that people of the Truth gain in this world can be carried through to the spirit world after death. Our organization provides clear teachings about the other world, and if you study these, it is unlikely that you will search for the kind of happiness that is limited to the material world only. My message does not infer that you have to be miserable in this life in order to be happy in the next. There are religious groups that convey such a message, but we need to be careful not to plant fresh seeds of misery on our journey through life. It is my profound hope that people can achieve the greatest possible happiness in this world as well as in the other world. And I feel it is my responsibility to provide teachings of the Truth to achieve this aim.

As long as your happiness in this world is not achieved at the cost of the happiness of others, it will lead to happiness in the spirit world. The best kind of happiness is the one that brings happiness to others as well as to you. This is the sort of happiness I would like you to achieve in this world and to take with you when you return to the spirit world.

It is for this reason that I would like everyone to develop and prosper in their professions, without creating attachments or bringing pain to others, and to use the happiness they gain as a way of conveying the Truth to those around them. I also hope that all those who enter the priesthood can savor the experiences of true spiritual growth, a real sense of development, and ultimately, success as souls.

CREATING AN IDEAL WORLD ON EARTH

The Principle of Progress is a teaching that is eminently suited to modern society. In Buddhist terms, this teaching deals with the building of a Buddha land, in other words, a Utopia, here on Earth.

My ultimate aim is to turn this world into Utopia. If we are able to build an ideal society, it will result in the diminishment of Hell. True, even working together we may not eliminate Hell all at once, but our first step on this road is to cut off the nourishment that the spirits in Hell require. The vicious cycle of unfortunate and misguided souls constantly entering Hell goes on. If we want to prevent this, we have to turn our world into Utopia, in other words, a heavenly world. Once this is achieved, those spirits residing in Hell will begin to reflect on their lives and will gradually ascend to the heavenly realms.

First, we must turn our planet into an ideal world where the majority of people learn the Truth, explore Right Mind, and strive to practice the Principles of Happiness.

You should not think that your work has finished when you have found your own happiness. If this has been achieved through awakening to the Truth, it then becomes your duty to spread your happiness to others to change the whole of society. Heaven existing in the spirit world is not enough for God. God constantly wishes for our material world, which so often seems like a muddy pond and close to Hell, to turn into Utopia. With this goal in mind, many Great Guiding Spirits of Light, angels, and bodhisattvas are being reincarnated into the world. Here they make strenuous efforts to spread the Truth and save people, even though to do so means that they encounter great hardship.

Eventually, you will leave this world. This is when you will become truly aware of how much effort the angels from the heavenly realms have been making to help souls in incarnations in the earthly world. You will be amazed and quite unable to hold back tears of gratitude for their efforts. Angels continue to make painful and persistent efforts to help people on Earth walk the path of happiness. When you bear in mind how many human beings there are in this world, it becomes obvious how arduous and thankless their task really is. Now that we know all that angels do for us while we are living on Earth, those of us who are awakened to the Truth must constantly redouble our efforts to turn our planet into Utopia, into the land of God.

We must all make it our goal to sow the seeds of enlightenment, to practice giving love. Start now by making an effort towards creating a Utopia in the town or city where you live. You can help to transform your school, company, society, country, and the world so that your surroundings become filled with love and light. Even living amidst a happy family is a start, because if every family were blessed in this way, the journey towards Utopia will have begun. And your effort to increase light and brighten the world, once started, must continue for the remainder of your life here on Earth.

Inside us all is a divine candle. When you awaken to the Truth, that candle has been lit. If you keep its light to yourself, it will only ever represent a single, solitary flame. If, however, you spread that light to the people around you and help them light their own candles, there will be two lights, twenty, a thousand, and eventually a million, as all spread their light to those around them. The result would be astonishing, and light would flood out in all directions. Will you lose anything at all by spreading this light? No, not a thing, because despite all the other candles you help light, your own still burns steady and bright.

We need to begin right now – constantly doubling and redoubling our efforts to chase away darkness and brighten our world. This is the meaning of creating a land of God, Utopia on Earth.

CHAPTER 5

Creating Heaven on Earth

WHEN PEOPLE ASK ME what I think is the basic difference between humans and animals, my answer is that humans are capable of thinking of and embracing an ideal. It is this quality that can guide our species to such heights. This is why so many religions preach that "Man is the lord of all creation" or "Human beings are closest to God in all creation."

If you fail to recognize your ideals, or lose your ability to strive for them, it can rightfully be suggested that you lose out on life. If, on the other hand, you continue to embrace an ideal no matter what difficulties you encounter and despite any amount of work necessary on the way, you will be a winner each and every day of your life. This show of inner strength is proof of your efforts and victories, regardless of the outer results.

PERSONAL HAPPINESS AND PUBLIC HAPPINESS

At Happy Science, we have been researching two specific concepts in relation to and as a basic foundation of my theory of Utopia. These are "happiness as an end" and "science as a means," which inspired the naming of the organization – Happy Science. To state it at its most basic, we are trying to find the answer to the question: "What do we need in order to attain happiness and what is the best way to go about it?" But perhaps, first, it would be quite valid for you to ask, "What do you actually mean by happiness?"

Happiness comes in two distinct forms: personal happiness and public happiness. Personal happiness refers to the contentment and peace of mind of an individual whereas public happiness applies it to society as a whole. What we at Happy Science seek is both forms of happiness, and this indicates what our proposed Utopia is all about. We aim to create a society in which each individual is overflowing with personal fulfillment, contentment, and joy, and also a world in which this state of mind is not confined to some, but can be enjoyed by absolutely everyone.

The best analogy I can think of is one that is close to the heart of all Japanese people. All of us have an overwhelming love of cherry trees, which each spring burst forth into a multitude of blossoms. These flowers do not appear one at a time, but all together, providing a spectacle that lifts the spirit and gladdens the eye. The flowering of the cherry epitomizes the beauty of April, but it isn't any single tree that makes the spectacle so wonderful. It is the fact that all cherry trees come into blossom at the same time, demonstrating the beauty of harmony.

We can look to the cherry tree to explain the idea of personal and public happiness. Each tree concentrates on putting forth its own flowers simultaneously, which is analogous to the attainment of happiness as an individual. The fact that all cherry trees bloom at the same time is a perfect metaphor for public happiness. Without all the cherry trees that bedeck our gardens and the countryside, Japan would be cheerless and empty in April, just as surely as no society can be a true Utopia if love does not exist everywhere, at the same instant.

It is perfectly possible to seek out our own happiness, but we will only achieve the springtime of humanity when each of us shows genuine affection, compassion, and happiness in pursuit of a greater happiness shared by the whole world. One of my purposes here is to tell you that it is time for spring to arrive, today. It is our cue to create a Utopia, and bring this season of warmth to all of humankind.

There is no better time than right now for a utopian world to blossom. A cherry tree cannot make its flowers bloom in summer, autumn, or winter; only in spring do all the factors combine to allow the tree to bloom. Likewise, only when we combine our resources, when God wills us to do so, can we realize Heaven on Earth, the true Utopia we seek. It is important to remind ourselves of the changing seasons when we think about Utopia and the actualization of happiness within it, and remember to step back and notice the larger scheme of things.

Happiness Comes from Enlightenment

You might quite reasonably ask, "Why are two kinds of happiness necessary?" To address this question, I will first talk about personal happiness. When is it that we feel happy? Is it when we are satisfied in some way, when we laugh heartily, or when we win the respect of others? The truth is that there are differences in the level of happiness people feel under differing circumstances. Some people are happy and satisfied as long as they can obtain their daily needs for sustaining life. But we at Happy Science strive towards a more elevated happiness. This happiness we seek to achieve is the highest form of personal happiness: the achievement of enlightenment. We regard anything short of this as a happiness derived *on the way to* enlightenment.

It might be suggested that personal enlightenment is synonymous with ultimate personal happiness. But why should this be the case? How and why does enlightenment lead to happiness? The first reason is that for people who live here, in our material world, true enlightenment is hard to obtain. It is the way of our world that people take delight in obtaining something that is difficult to get. Only when you have striven hard to attain enlightenment does the spiritual training you have received in your life become worthwhile.

At the same time, it is enlightenment that changes personal happiness into public happiness. This is the second reason why enlightenment brings us happiness. Enlightenment consists of two facets. I have already described the first facet, personal happiness, which is derived from the experience of personal inner joy. Once you have attained the happiness of personal enlightenment, you cannot avoid having altruistic thoughts and this results in your personal joy being passed on to others. That is the second facet of enlightenment. The very act of working towards enlightenment means being aware of your mission regarding humankind, together with an understanding of where you came from and where you are heading. When you awaken to the original mission of human life, you can no longer sit back and watch. Taking action becomes unavoidable and inevitable.

Once aware of your mission in life, you will head in a very specific direction, towards overwhelming goodwill and altruism. If you begin to feel you have no alternative but to love others, if you want to have a positive influence on the world around you and make everyone you meet happy, this is pure altruism. At its most basic, enlightenment is "awareness of the mission of humanity" and also "awareness of your personal mission." Enlightenment leads to good, and ultimately, the actualization of public happiness, happiness for everyone.

It is inevitable that at some time in the future you will leave this world. When you are back in the spirit world and assessing what you achieved during your earthly incarnation, you will be filled with thoughts about how you did or did not contribute to the greater good, and all souls will regret some lack in how much they contributed to public happiness. No matter how dynamic or passionate your life was, or the fact that you were deeply intellectual or contemplative, your soul will not be satisfied if you know you failed to lead as many people as possible to happiness. You can never do enough and your work will never be complete.

Even Angels of Light shed tears of regret after they leave Earth and look back at the life they lived there. No matter how much they achieved, they will still ask, "Why did I live such a life? It could have been different. I should have loved more people and helped them to achieve their dreams. Look how little I managed to achieve."

Many Angels of Light, and others who are on their way to becoming one, are living among you. In time, many of you will experience a spiritual awakening, recall the mission that you promised to fulfill, and start on the path to learning and conveying the Truth. You will eventually help guide a great many people to Truth. But you must remember that even though many awakened angels might safely find the path to their calling, at the end of life when they glance back at the distance they traveled, all of them will feel disappointment. It is therefore very important that, rather than looking at your life from the point of view of the present, you should try to examine your current life from the point at which you leave the world. You should consider how many years you might have left and how far you still have to go. With every passing hour, you must be determined to work on improving yourself.

If you think in this way, I am sure you will find passion welling up inside you. If this is not the case, you might be failing in your ultimate objective as a human being. Live a positive life and continue to offer as much courage and light to the greatest number of people possible.

Reviewing your life in this way will bring about a form of spiritual awakening, an experience that I would like to share with more people. I created Happy Science so I can offer more people the chance to experience this through our seminars. This was the original purpose of the organization, which must be kept alive.

QUIET HAPPINESS AND ACTIVE HAPPINESS

There are two varieties of happiness in general: quiet happiness, which emphasizes satisfaction; and active happiness, which represents progress and development. With quiet happiness, we know how to be content, but active happiness gives us joy in the knowledge that we are growing and moving forward. Imagine that you are sitting with a cup of tea and relaxing at the end of a busy day. You may be content that things have gone well or feeling pleased that your family members are healthy and fulfilled. The happiness you feel at this moment is a familiar form of happiness that is based on satisfaction. There is nothing essentially wrong with this state of mind, but it is hardly dynamic.

Now think about the many people in history who viewed happiness from a more proactive and dynamic point of view. Such people were leaders, who used all their courage, strength, and skill to lead others as a result of the overwhelming light of goodwill and wise judgment within them. These individuals made their time on Earth the turning points of history. They let everyone know that the happiness of humanity can never lie in inactivity or passiveness; rather, it is found in what is active and vigorous. Active happiness constantly aspires to achieve greater progress and improvement. There is an extraordinary power that can be derived from the type of happiness that focuses on progress and growth. You have only to look at the historical accomplishments of many respected figures to discover that a remarkable power infused their work and that it always added to the progress of humanity and improved the lot of everyone.

So, which sort of happiness is best? Is it quiet happiness or active happiness? Doubtless you, like everyone else, have been torn between these two alternatives at some time in your life and it could be that you find it difficult to know which of these alternatives represents the best and most important way to be happy.

Religious leaders from ancient times on have told us that truth lies between two extremes. If you find yourself attracted to two conflicting possibilities, in the end you may have to admit that both have something to offer you and that each may be necessary in its own way. Bearing this in mind, quiet and active happiness might be compared to the brake and gas pedal of a car, respectively. Like the way the brake and gas pedal affect the car, these two kinds of happiness affect you when you are driving the vehicle of life.

People sometimes get highly excited when they live their lives at a frenetic pace. Such individuals need to be reminded now and again about the happiness that is to be gained from simple contentment. The problem is that these people are so busy and active and live so frenetically that they can tread on the dreams of others and make them sad, often without realizing that this is taking place. In other words, in their anxiety to devote themselves totally to their own vision, they actually become the source of the suffering of others.

Fortunately, life has a self-regulating mechanism, which brings trials and setbacks to individuals who have become excessively self-engrossed. Hard times in life offer them a chance to remember that there is a type of happiness that can also be found in the present moment.

On the other hand, those who know how to be personally content are inclined to get themselves into a rut. They may live their lives aimlessly. They need to be reminded that they too have a gas pedal in their vehicle of life. We need to point out to them that if they forget to apply the gas pedal now and again, they will be unable to move forward. Such people may feel safe staying still because they might think they are on a country road but often life is like an expressway. They might be content to sit in the middle of the road but what about all the cars behind them, honking wildly to move on? They are like egotists. Despite the fact that there is a need for development and progress, such people continue to block the way. When others push for a positive life and want things to happen, they insist on doing everything in their own slow way.

The analogy of the cars reminds me of the Academy Award–winning film *Rain Man,* in which Dustin Hoffman played the role of an autistic man called Raymond who is a perfectionist and also quite inflexible. In one scene of the film, Raymond is crossing a road at the pedestrian lights when the "Don't walk" signal flashes on in red. Instead of moving on quickly to the other side of the road, Raymond takes the command literally and remains where he is, right in the middle of the intersection. No matter how many cars blow their horns and no matter how many drivers shout at Raymond, he refuses to move. The scene was amusing, but it brought me to thinking that there are many people in life who are rather like Raymond. These are the people who indulge in the form of happiness epitomized by self-contentment, often to the exclusion of the comfort and happiness of those around them.

Those who tend to be energetic and live their lives at a breakneck pace need to be reminded how good quiet happiness can be, whereas people who are content with being stuck in a rut and who live their lives without any clear goals or objectives need to be told that the gas pedal is important too. Everyone needs to learn how to use the brake and the accelerator at the right time for the right situation to function well as a member of society. If traffic is moving slowly, you have to be able to operate both of them accordingly. You also need to keep in mind that traffic conditions for a given road change frequently, depending on the time of day and the day of the week. In our search for happiness, each of us needs to seek the harmony of embracing opposites, yet without relying exclusively on either.

The Universal Truth, the Truth of God

To achieve an adequate balance of the two forms of happiness, we need some method that allows us to attain personal happiness while practicing public happiness. In fact, personal happiness should lead naturally to greater harmony with the rest of society and contribute to the improvement and evolution of humanity as a whole, which is what public happiness is. This brings us to the Universal Truth that has been preached throughout the ages. Universal Truth, the Truth of God, is directly aimed at achieving great harmony between private and public happiness. This is also my theory of Utopia.

Actually, to some extent, Universal Truth is already at work within society. The morals most of us take for granted and the views that define how we live as human beings are not necessarily the legacies of religion or philosophy alone.

If we are brought up properly, we learn many of these automatically, even if our parents are never religious. Basic rules such as "You should not steal," and "You should not use violence against others," together with the understanding that "You should not break a contract when you have given your word," are reflected in the laws of most nations. They are, to a great extent, the result of a consensus of humanity as a whole.

In reality, these moral imperatives all originate in Universal Truth. Without them, our world would exist in a state of chaos, and chaos is the exact opposite of the order that is God. The existence of these moral imperatives contributes to maintaining the happiness of the greatest number of people possible. That is why Universal Truth, which is the essence of all religious truths, should never be driven into the corners of the minds of human beings. It is a wide and glorious path and in fact the central path of our lives.

Happy Science is working every day to inform as many people as possible that the Truths of God that I preach are the Truths of the cosmic universe and the Truths that have existed throughout the history of humankind. These Truths represent the central path for all things who exist in the universe, from which all other paths originate, including the paths of growth and prosperity. I sincerely hope that all of my readers, rather than simply looking at Universal Truth with curiosity or as a side issue, will take pride in studying it and realize that by doing so they are walking straight and true on this golden path. It cannot be marginalized and it must remain at the very core of our understanding of life. It is actually the greatest path of life that anyone can ever choose.

Let us move on now to principles that reconcile personal happiness and public happiness without adversely affecting either. This is the starting point of Utopian thought. It is the essence of Universal Truth.

THE CREATION OF SOULS

What is the driving force to create a Utopia in which an individual's happiness and the happiness of society as a whole can be realized? Where can we find the essence of this force? I would like to discuss this from two standpoints. The first one is epitomized by the question "Why does a desire to become happy well up inside us?" and the second by the question "Why is the happiness of society as a whole necessary?"

One of the reasons an individual wishes to become happy lies in an urge within the soul. When we enter this world, our souls do not entirely forget that they split off from the Primordial God. Deep in the recesses of our inner selves, these memories linger. There is an element within our souls that sometimes calls for peace and at other times urges progress and action. Such feelings are possible because of the nostalgia our soul feels for its origin.

I am absolutely sure that each and every person reading this book wants to become happy and to maintain this state into the future. You would probably also admit, without much prompting, that being happy is a delight and that it lifts your soul. You can be sure that others feel exactly the same way and that what pleases you will also please them. In the Christian Bible, there is a saying that is as true now as it was two thousand years ago: "Do unto others as you would have them do unto you." If we all stop to think about it for a moment, this innate desire to be of assistance to other people and to help them all we can is inherent in all peoples. It is the core of the golden rule of life. If everything you do only serves to displease others and make them unhappy, the golden rule cannot hold true.

It is a curious fact about our world that people seem to live separately, but in reality, the souls of all humans are connected to each other by God's neurons. In other words part of God's very essence and thinking exists in each one of us. This situation is not static; it can be compared to the blood vessels in a human body. These blood vessels of God are invisible to the human eye but nevertheless they split and spread throughout the entire universe, like a great net that exists everywhere. This mesh of God's essence isn't available to us only; it holds all elements and kinds of life on Earth together. This is the reason that, although we may sometimes think it is the case, we are never separated but are part of one great whole.

Our souls remember vaguely a time that is unimaginably distant. There was a moment when our souls split from the Primordial God. It happened as far back as trillions of years in the past when one spot out there in the vastness of space, which was itself part of God's consciousness, suddenly exploded into myriad particles of light, each possessing its own individuality as well as its connection with God. These innumerable flickers of light became our souls. This is why it is said that a human being is "a child of God" or alternatively, "a child of light."

Please do not confuse this event with those occasions when a star explodes or is broken into pieces. The myriad lights that came into existence as our souls were not comprised of physical matter; they were entirely spiritual in composition. Seen from a spiritual perspective, this magnificent event represented a massive diffusion of energy from the spirit world that spread throughout the whole universe.

As each part of God's energy spread farther and farther from its point of origin, it remained connected to the whole by means of what we could refer to as an artery, like a stout blood vessel. When this occurred, these main arteries became the basic source of energy for the star clusters existing throughout the universe. One "artery" runs through to the Milky Way, which flows through to the Solar System. As each part of the energy spread, it branched out into smaller arteries and capillaries, but the ultimate connections were never severed. In this way, the entire universe remains connected as a vast network of spiritual energy.

This was not a once-and-for-all happening. It went through several phases. The oldest of these took place twenty billion years ago and the most recent spiritual diffusions of our own galaxy happened about three billion years ago. This is one of the facts of the universe you will not read in any book dealing with science; in reality, it is the secret of the universe. At various periods, at intervals of billions of years, various cores of spiritual energy formed in different parts of the universe, each expanding and creating a new net of life, new family trees, wherever its influence was felt.

As one billion, two billion, and then three billion years passed, around and along the smaller arteries and capillaries of the net of God's energy – this grand family tree – various life forms came into existence on the planets.

When these various life forms came about, God did not intend them to take on fixed forms immediately. All sorts of plants and animals that came into existence on Earth and elsewhere were destined to change and diversify. Through an immensely long period, elements of life evolved into something more progressive and more suited to their surroundings and purpose. As this suggests, the first forms of life made possible by the presence of God's energy were simple, but with the passing of time they developed into more complex life forms of the sort we see around us today.

Because we are born of God, we carry the same nature as God. It is a profound and beautiful fact that we are the children of God because our souls once comprised, and still do comprise, God. This is the absolute Truth about our souls and their origin.

Being children of God, it follows that we also have the same objectives. These are progress and harmony, the two major objectives that God established when creating the universe. We carry these two objectives at the core of our souls as an inner ideal. This is the reason we have an urge within our souls towards evolution – a desire to progress and develop – and harmony in the form of peace and beauty. The reason we strive towards peace and progress or harmony and development is directly due to the fact that we are all children of God. Our pursuit of happiness is the irrefutable proof of our oneness with God. We are life forms entrusted with sacred missions. The great objectives we have been set lie at the very root of our lives, and the light of God shines in us all.

The principles of progress and harmony are not confined to all living things on Earth, but they also apply far beyond our little planet to sentient races throughout the universe. The level of progress we have achieved here, however, is not the same everywhere. Even from the same starting point, life has evolved much more in some regions of the universe than in others. In other words, some are racing ahead, while others lag behind. There are very developed areas of space and others that are still primitive.

In the main, we on Earth remain ignorant of the many diverse races that exist in the universe. You can be sure that some of these have visited our planet. For those who choose to look carefully enough there is plenty of proof, but for the moment their presence among us remains generally unrecognized.

In fact, the US government already knows about the existence of extraterrestrial life. The United States Air Force has a great amount of information about them and has communicated with them.

Advanced forms of civilization on other planets are far ahead of ours on Earth. Some are two thousand years ahead of us, or even as much as six thousand years. In fact, beings from other planets are already living on Earth with us. One very large group came from a group of planets called Pleiades, and they currently form the majority of extraterrestrials who come to Earth.

They did not migrate to Earth in their physical forms as a group, however. They migrated in their soul forms, and incarnated on Earth in human form. They are actually planning for an official physical migration in the future, and those who have been born on Earth are making preparations for it.

This migration began at the turn of the century, and people on Earth will eventually begin to notice this fact. It will begin slowly in the twenty-first century, and will continue on in greater numbers through the twenty-fifth, twenty-eighth, and all the way to the thirtieth century. They will be coming to Earth in massive numbers.

Similarly, some of the older inhabitants of Earth will leave the planet; some of them will move out spiritually in their soul form, while others will physically go from here to outer space.

They will choose to migrate either to more advanced societies to learn new things, or developing ones that offer more creative possibilities. This will happen during the next ten centuries on Earth, and readers of this book will be born on Earth at least once or twice within that period and see this happening. Plans and preparations for this began a long time ago in the spirit world.

As I have already stated, the essential nature of human beings originated from God. We were originally part of him that separated, and that was how we were created in His likeness. This is why we are all children of God. This is true of all other beings who live on other planets; they are our "space brothers" who also live by God's laws, including of course, the laws of progress and harmony.

The grand spirit who has achieved the highest level of spirituality beyond Earth is always considering the differences in the pace at which each inhabited planet and its life forms evolve, and is thinking about what can be done to bring greater development and prosperity to the rest of creation, and how to achieve it efficiently. The situation is quite complex, but as an example, the grand spirit will assess spirits on Earth who have already attained a degree of enlightenment and consider how to help them grow further. He thinks about what sort of region would be most appropriate for their soul training, and whether ten, twenty, or a hundred incarnations on Earth would really benefit them or whether it might be better for their soul evolution to recommence further incarnations in a completely different part of the universe. Thus, the idea of evolution and harmony – progress and harmony – is applied not only to our little world. There is a great being who sees everything from a broader perspective, from far above Earth, and puts the conclusions into practice.

Then why is it that humanity, the nature of which is to search for personal happiness, needs also to aim at public happiness and the well-being of all life forms? The answer lies in the fact that all the innumerable lights, the souls that were created so very long ago as part of the one and only God, have the same overriding desire to return to their source, to be once again part of God. It is as if we are all children, sent off on some great educational trip, constantly seeking to go home to our parent, loaded with souvenirs of personal happiness, and eager to share joy with each other. This is how public happiness is created. It is important to hold this analogy in your mind because this great homecoming is, itself, the movement of creating Utopia or the land of God on Earth. This is the most earnest wish and the ultimate goal of Happy Science.

We have seen that human beings were created, with their countless sentient relatives, as a result of splitting off from God, and because they did, their combined souls carry a great purpose. The ultimate manifestation of this purpose is the desire of all souls that originated from the "one and only

God" to return to the "one and only God," a manifestation of which in our world is to strive to create a Utopia on Earth. The euphoria you enjoyed when you once existed as one with God remained and part of the instructions given to the newly created souls was to recreate this same heavenly euphoria wherever they went.

Let us suppose that a great number of people who are presently studying the teachings of Happy Science become happy as a result of their enlightenment. They might say, "We are really happy and we are delighted to be together." Would I be pleased about this? Well, yes, but only up to a point. I would instruct them that no matter how happy they are to be together and to be achieving their own enlightenment, their work is certainly not over. They should not be content but must retain an overwhelming desire to pass on their own joy to others. My message to the enlightened is to help others attain happiness. Pass on the buds of happiness in other places, help other people's happiness bloom just as surely as you have found them and watched your own come to flower. I would say to everyone, "You may be truly happy and contented to be united in your small group, but each and every one of you should become a seed that can germinate and grow to create the same happiness everywhere." This is a small version of what is happening all over the universe.

Ultimately, I would like to say happiness in a small group is just happiness within a limited frame. Each individual's happiness within this limited frame can amplify on its own, however. Happiness expanding in this way invites yet more happiness. At Happy Science, we are constantly putting this concept into practice.

THE MISSION OF HUMANKIND

At this point, I think we need to reconsider the mission of humankind. Why are we given different personalities? Why should we be born into this world, undergo spiritual training, and then return to the other world? After all, God, who created the entire cosmos, conceived the laws of the universe, in order to combine two apparently conflicting objectives. These were, "infinite evolution" and "great harmony." God expected human beings to play a role as practitioners in the laws of the universe. As a result, it has been necessary for God to preach the laws of the universe as they apply to human society. These are the Truths that the Great Guiding Spirits of Light have striven to establish on Earth, throughout history. In short, the Truth that we have been exploring is a guidebook that helps us learn and experience the laws of the universe, which are the Dharma, the laws, that aim to actualize evolution and harmony on Earth.

In governing the universe, God entrusted each spirit group of each planet with the implementation of the laws God had conceived. Therefore, like the innumerable other spirit groups that exist throughout the universe, the inhabitants on Earth hold responsibility for its operation, as one autonomous community among many others in the cosmos.

God established the basic governing principle that each spirit group would be a self-governing community, hoped that the more advanced spirits would strive to become representatives of God's Will, and entrusted them with the responsibility and leadership of looking after the spirit group. In a way, this system enabled these advanced spirits to further grow and evolve ever closer to God.

The task of striving to create a Utopia has been given to the inhabitants of each planet, and all manner of people are putting tremendous effort into making their own worlds radiant and fit for the laws of God. All individuals in a given society are responsible for building Heaven in their own world. Their jobs or occupations contribute to this goal, and each household is a perfect foundation on which to build a Utopia.

Much as different countries have always been in a race to become the world's best nation, many civilizations on other planets scattered throughout the universe are striving towards improvement and advancement, and competing to make their own planet shine the brightest of all.

So, the grandest and most worthy mission of the human race on Earth is to achieve the highest possible progress and advancement, with the greatest harmony. To accomplish this mission and actualize the ideals that God has set before us, the creation of Utopia on Earth, while still making the most of our individuality, we are expected to work together as souls with different skills and personalities. The fulfillment of the ideal that is Utopia is the greatest task assigned to each one of us.

In God's grand scheme, planets strive eternally for further progress and harmony. On Earth, the human race is racing towards the same goal, and to facilitate this undertaking, certain individuals have been assigned special roles. In the spirit world, there are many realms that relate specifically to these roles. Among these is the ninth dimension, where saviors and messiahs are to be found. Then there is the realm of Great Angels and Great Guiding Spirits in the eighth dimension and the realm of Angels of Light in the seventh dimension, the realm of Guiding Spirits. The upper levels of the sixth dimension are designated for spirits who specialize in a field.

The Great Angels and Angels of Light, known in Buddhist terms as the tathagatas and bodhisattvas, gradually came to these positions after countless reincarnations of goodness and service. It is these souls who have constantly striven to create Utopia, to bring God's Heaven to Earth. Time and again they shouldered the responsibility of leadership and underwent unbelievable hardships and travails on behalf of humanity. Eventually, their own efforts and accomplishments made them into Great Angels and Angels of Light.

The Angels of Light are like the directors of motion pictures or the conductors of symphony orchestras. Their role is to direct the actors and actresses and help bring out their unique characteristics, tap into their strengths, and harmonize these separate individuals to form a beautiful story.

Since many, if not all, of the Great Angels and Angels of Light have achieved their status and position after countless incarnations on Earth, it stands to reason that ordinary souls can gradually increase their capacity as spiritual leaders and teachers until they too become Angels of Light or Great Angels. To achieve this state of leadership, you need to have many accomplishments towards creating Utopia on Earth. If you make sufficient efforts, your spiritual maturity and light will increase; whereas, if you neglect your discipline, the light you offer to the world will gradually diminish. And, just as any soul can reach this elevated status, Great Angels and Angels of Light can lose that status if they fail to offer the guidance, leadership, and level of enlightenment necessary. Everyone is given the same opportunities to progress, and in the spirit world, we are rewarded fairly according to our efforts. This is a fundamental principle.

The account we eventually have to offer of our actions, our progress, and our ultimate enlightenment is not only dependent on the life we are living at this moment in time. We are also called to account for our actions in previous lives. Of course, we don't all know the details of our previous lives – who we were, where we lived, or what we achieved – but blow-by-blow accounts aren't necessary. This is because what you are now represents an accumulation of all your past lives. Everything you have ever been is encapsulated in your nature today. If you want to change your future, you can make a new start now. As noted, everyone has an equal opportunity. Your starting point can be anywhere, and you will be fairly and impartially rewarded according to your effort. Nobody can tell you in this life what the ultimate judgment for your soul will be, but each of us has to be prepared to accept the outcome. The existence of this immutable principle is a great blessing to humanity. It has allowed us to undertake soul training for billions of years. The fact that God's law is impartial and just makes it worthwhile for us to continue to exert our efforts.

THE PRINCIPLE OF PROGRESS – ACQUIRING TRUTH AND PRACTICING ALTRUISM

The central objective of all humanity is to aim for nothing less than to improve the terrestrial spirit group as a whole and to create great harmony on Earth. Since our objectives are straightforward and noble, it should not be too difficult to establish how we can achieve our goal.

The method for creating Utopia can be summed up in two principles: the principle of progress and the principle of harmony. These are the foundations on which God's Heaven on Earth will be built.

The principle of progress is a way of attaining personal happiness. This means an increase in the amount of light each individual soul emits, together with an improvement of the spiritual state of each soul. This is the same process as the one for attaining enlightenment. The ultimate goal of this principle is that every soul should attain enlightenment and then improve upon it. The more enlightenment you attain, the greater will be the amount of spiritual light you shed upon the world. As a result, you can become more influential and achieve greater and more elevated tasks. If you find this difficult to believe, I would like to set you a test. If you make a wholehearted effort for only a year, the difference will be amazing. And, once you have experienced it, you will understand it. I would like you to learn what a massive change you can make in yourself by awakening to the Truth. And as you progress, the spiritual light you emit will increase, until it touches everyone with whom you come into contact.

Those who shine like the sun and offer their light to a great number of people become Angels of Light and Guiding Spirits of Light. On the other hand, people who think about nothing but taking from others and who care only about themselves eventually become messengers of darkness. It is as simple as that. For this reason, as discussed in an earlier chapter, I ask you to change your perspective. Stop thinking about yourself and pay more attention to those around you. Live your life for the sake of others and refine yourself by studying their needs.

There are two minimum requirements for enlightenment. The first is to acquire the correct knowledge of the Truth. You cannot claim that you have attained enlightenment unless you have a clear and concise understanding of the Truth. Unfortunately, the experience that one person normally gains through even several decades of life on Earth is not sufficient in itself to be called enlightenment. In order to embrace enlightenment, you need to study thoroughly the wisdom of humanity that has been accumulated in the past. It's not something that people can discover all on their own. You must learn the established Truth with modesty. A humble willingness to learn the teachings will speed up your spiritual progress by as much as several decades.

For this purpose, Happy Science provides various seminars and training programs, and I hope these will become opportunities for you to study the Truth. I encourage you to allow yourself to proceed at a pace that works for you and view these programs as opportunities to acquire and deepen your knowledge of the Truth.

In what is known as "direct spiritual awakening," the resulting enlightenment supposedly cannot be expressed in words. Some people claim to have attained enlightenment in this way, but if you cannot perceive the meaning of your existence, the mission of your life, and the purpose of your living in the current age, you cannot claim that you have achieved enlightenment. I have to point out that those making such a claim can hardly be said to have attained an enlightenment worthy of the age in which they were born.

The enlightenment of a hundred, five hundred, or a thousand years ago cannot be the same as that of today. You must try to grasp the best enlightenment that can be achieved in this current age. To do that, you need to study humbly what has been accumulated as wisdom. Those who do only as they like in pursuit of enlightenment have existed throughout the ages, but this is not a desirable approach. What you base your thoughts and actions on is important.

The second requirement in attaining enlightenment is the practice of giving love. Those who do not try to love others, nurture those around them, or sympathize with other human beings cannot be called enlightened people. Regrettably, very few people are aware of this. You probably encounter numerous people in your work or your community. What percentage of them takes delight in having altruistic thoughts and putting these into practice? How many of them take spontaneous action and talk honestly and compassionately to those around them? Certainly, there are some people who behave as if they were showing love to others, but quite a few of them are actually seeking ways to benefit themselves. How many people do you know whose genuine quest in life is to love others?

It is the most earnest desire of God that you turn yourself into such an individual – loving, caring, and compassionate. To follow the Will and the laws of God, there is no alternative but to become such a person. If the whole world is filled with people who truly care for those around them, the world automatically becomes a Utopia. I hope you will join me on the road to creating this Heaven on Earth.

In creating the perfect world, a Utopia, knowledge and love will be our tools. The acquiring of the correct knowledge of the Truth and the practice of giving love are the minimum requirements for attaining enlightenment. Making an effort in these two areas is what the Principle of Progress means.

THE PRINCIPLE OF HARMONY — TOLERANCE AND FORGIVENESS

Tolerance and forgiveness are important to the principle of harmony. Tolerance is especially important in religious terms. Please remember, however, that being tolerant does not mean accepting or approving of what is wrong. You need to discriminate right from wrong. But it is also important to wait patiently for those who follow incorrect religious paths to awaken to the Truth. You need to give them time and continue to encourage them without becoming impatient or giving up. This is the true meaning of tolerance.

Another important aspect of the principle of harmony is forgiveness. To understand forgiveness is to believe in the good nature of all people. Forgiveness means believing and praying that those who eventually realize their mistakes will find their way forward through repentance, start a new life, and begin to shine. To accept that human nature is basically good and to pray that the goodness within all people will manifest itself in the end is the essence of forgiveness.

Furthermore, to understand the true meaning of tolerance and forgiveness, you have to experience both self-reflection and prayer. Those who have not reflected upon themselves or offered sincere prayers cannot understand tolerance or forgiveness in the truest sense. Accordingly, besides studying

Truth as a mere intellectual pursuit, you have to apply the Truth you have learned in everyday life. At the same time, you need to reflect upon yourself to make certain you are really practicing the Truth on every occasion.

Prayer is also important. In your prayers, give blessings to others. Pray that you might improve yourself in order to be of service to society and that you might make the most of your life, your abilities, and your talents for the benefit of many, instead of merely for self-interest. The methods of connecting directly with God, through self-reflection and prayer, become a power that actively and strongly promotes the task of creating Utopia.

Realizing Utopia in our material world requires not only human effort, but also the support of Divine Spirits in the spirit world. Always bear in mind that maintaining your connection with them is also a major step on the road to creating Utopia.

In conclusion, through the virtues of tolerance and forgiveness, creating Utopia on Earth by achieving harmony among people who aim for progress is a major assignment for Happy Science and for all people who seek enlightenment. This is our organization's ultimate goal. As for each individual's effort, you have to use the tools of wisdom and love. It is important to pay your respects constantly to higher beings in the spirit world who have powers far beyond ours in the material world. It is also your duty to improve yourself so that you can receive their power. This is why you need to practice self-reflection, meditation, and prayer.

Through the mysterious and amazing experience of connecting with God and with Divine Spirits, I hope you will join me in making Utopia on Earth a reality.

CHAPTER 6

The Moment of Truth

A N EXTREMELY MATERIALISTIC CULTURE has developed around the world, making Earth a convenient place to live. I have no intention of rejecting worldly conveniences and I certainly do not suggest we should return to some primitive age. There is one thing we must never forget amid our progress and technology, however, and that is faith. First and foremost, I want to create a world that is supported by a backbone of faith.

When people lose sight of faith, a fundamental principle that governs the universe, when they become concerned with trivial details, they get lost and start to make mistakes. Mistakes made by one or two people can be overlooked, but when numerous people begin to go wrong, massive negative reactions develop. Faith is what we need as our foundation in order to prevent hundreds of millions or even billions of people from going wrong.

Believe in the existence of the Primordial God and God's compassionate gaze. The universe is certainly not without purpose or guidance. The universe is vast. It stretches to infinity, a place of countless shining stars, which in relation to the size of the universe are nothing but tiny dots of light. There are living beings throughout the cosmos and a great Creator looks down upon all of them with compassionate eyes.

When the universe was created, first there was Will. Just as no child can be born in the absence of parents, there would be no universe if Will had not existed first. The universe came into being because Will existed and because that same Will wished to nurture the living beings that would evolve here. This parent-like Will can be referred to as the Will of the Primordial God who casts a gaze upon us from a distant place. To God's eyes, this three-dimensional universe is nothing more than a tiny speck, although those living on Earth perceive the cosmos as vast and boundless. It was Will that allowed the cosmos to come into existence and without it the Big Bang could never have occurred in a physical sense. It is possible to offer all kinds of explanations for the resulting chemical reaction, but the truth is that Will existed first. Ultimately, Will also created this phenomenal world in which we all live. When Will focused on a specific point, it materialized into form. This is how all things in the material, three-dimensional world, came into being.

Believe in the existence of the Primordial God. Accept that Primordial God created vast numbers of angels and Guiding Spirits of Light to convey God's Will. Believe God has always guided numerous beings, including humanity. This is what you need to know and accept in order to prevent yourself from becoming misguided and from heading in the wrong direction.

FAITH — BELIEVING IN GOD'S LAWS

No matter how advanced science and technology become, there is a point beyond which human beings can never go. We cannot change the principles that construct the universe. Human beings may come up with the most wonderful inventions and might have numerous new ideas, but we can never change the principles of God. This is because the principles come from the Primordial Will.

When I say this, I am not only referring to the physical laws that govern three-dimensional space, but also the principles that govern human life. According to these principles, although we human beings exist only in a physical form in this world, we were originally the inhabitants of the world beyond our material limitations. From that place, our true home, we were born on Earth, to undergo spiritual refinement. This is not only true for human beings, but also for animals and plants. In Heaven, many flowers bloom, including flowers that no longer exist on Earth, blossoms that grew and flourished in the distant past. Heaven also contains animals that have become extinct in our world but still live in the other world. That is because this other world, Heaven, is our true home. This is an immutable principle.

It may be incomprehensible to you if the grounds of your reasoning are based only on this world and you think that science and technology are omnipotent. You probably never learned about this at school. But simply because you do not know about it does not mean the other world does not exist. The fact is that you live in a universe that has this dual structure. What is more, the material world and the spirit world do not exist independently of each other. They overlap and influence each other.

We live in this vast universe and we go through a long and continuous series of reincarnations, so we should not perceive time and distance based on the limited perspective of just a single life that merely spans a few decades. We need to broaden our horizons and believe in the Primordial Being who created the grand cosmos, including the spirit world. We must also have faith in and believe in those who work to give guidance to people as God's representatives on Earth. This sort of faith needs to become the very basis of all our lives.

From now on, we have to devote ourselves to spreading the Truth throughout the entire world. This is especially important in countries where materialistic values predominate and in nations where a large percentage of the population disparage the spirit world and the concept of faith. We will fight against this ignorance. But this is not a fight simply for the sake of fighting; it is a combat on behalf of love. Beyond this, it is a fight for the sake of Truth. Numerous people live false lives because they don't know the Truth. As a result, such individuals must spend tens or hundreds of years after death in great pain in Hell. If people knew of the Truth at an early stage in their incarnations, they would make fewer mistakes.

LOVE – BECOMING GOD'S MESSENGERS

The ideal attitude when living in this era is, first, to have faith, and second, to live your life giving and expressing love. We have to create a world in which love is present everywhere. The great being we refer to as God has a heart filled with love and compassion. This heart nourishes and guides people, so as children of God, we too must live in love and compassion.

As I have illustrated throughout this book, the sad fact is that many crave love, but few are willing to offer it. This is the nature of the world in which we live. If people helped each other, they would be sure to live in happiness. Conversely, because so many try to take from each other all the time, happiness eludes them. It saddens me to look out on this sort of world. Only if people turn their perspectives around and change their thinking will they be able to find true happiness.

Real love is not gained from taking it from others; it is gained from giving it. We need to offer love to everyone because we are God's children. God embodies love and compassion, so leading a life of offering love is proof that you are a child of God. There are many philosophies related to love. But the simplest point is the most important. Taking love is nothing more than the attachment discussed in Buddhist teachings. So, rather than complaining about how little love you receive, think about how much you have loved others in your life, and how much you will love others in the future. This will become the driving force in creating an ideal world.

Instead of asking continually for others to do things on your behalf, ask yourself what you can do for them. It isn't difficult and you will find all the answers you need in your own heart. You must live your life in a way that gives unconditionally. I ask you to be like the Sun, which works tirelessly and never asks a penny for all its effort. In this way, Heaven will manifest on Earth.

ENLIGHTENMENT — KNOWING WHO YOU ARE

Enlightenment is another principle that I would like you to understand. The word "enlightenment" has Buddhist overtones, so you might think it is a conception relevant only to a particular religion. On the contrary, it is very important for everyone to have a true understanding of enlightenment. To put it simply, attaining enlightenment means awakening to the fact that there is more to human beings than their physical bodies: we have souls, and the mind, which is found in the core of the soul, is the control center of the entire body.

There are people who consider Buddhism to be atheism, materialism, or a religion that teaches that the soul and the spirit do not exist. These people cannot deny, however, that Buddhism acknowledges the existence of the mind. Some people argue that Buddhism teaches egolessness, and if there is no ego, that means the soul does not exist. However, even these critics cannot claim that the mind does not exist. And the truth is that the mind is, in fact, the essence of what the soul is. The essence of being human is the ability to alter our thoughts and to make choices and decisions based on our own free will. We are given personal freedom and can decide what to think. Many people simply have a mistaken view of the soul as a solid, three-dimensional thing. But in truth, what makes us, are the ideas and thoughts that come to us freely. These things are what make us who we are, and they continue to exist after our death and will be taken back with us to the other world.

In fact, when we return to the other world, we can take only our mind, the collection of our thoughts, with us.

There, the soul will retain its human form for as long as its memories are fresh. These gradually fade and the soul loses its resemblance to the human form. Eventually, the soul appears only as thoughts; only the will survives.

That is why we often find that ideas that are truly sublime last for long periods of time after the conceiver's death. The thoughts of those who did great deeds hundreds or even thousands of years ago are still present in the spirit world. Their noble deeds continue to influence a great many people on Earth to this day.

For instance, Jesus Christ lived thirty-three years on Earth, a relatively short life, but his work did not end when he left his physical body. His legacy is still alive and influencing people today. Shakyamuni Buddha left this world twenty-five hundred years ago. Some of you might wonder if people living so long ago could have said anything of worth, but the compassionate mind and the enlightenment the Buddha taught are still highly valued to this very day. This is a reflection of the mystery and wonder of the spirit world.

It is important to realize that those of us living on Earth are not merely flesh and blood. We are spiritual beings and our minds are the essence of our true selves. I am not referring to a mind that is in a state of delusion, but to the true essence of the human mind. If we want to achieve true happiness and enlightenment, it is necessary to change the way we think and see ourselves.

Consider: what are the thoughts you have every day? What have you been thinking about for the last year or for the last ten years? The level of your thoughts and awareness you have managed to attain while on Earth will determine the level of the world, the realm, you will return to after death. As I have explained throughout this book, when you make an effort and discipline yourself in attempts to become closer to God, your mind will be elevated and purified, and its brilliance will increase. If you have managed to live with the heart of a bodhisattva while you have been on Earth, after your death your soul will go to the seventh dimension, the world of bodhisattvas and nowhere else. You do not have to wait for the moment of your death to discover whether you are going to Heaven or Hell. It is possible to know where your soul is bound while you are still alive.

Therefore, increasing your level of enlightenment is a way of designing a better plan for the future. It will determine the sort of life you will live henceforth and it will awaken you to your true mission. This is why raising your level of enlightenment is crucially important.

I would like you to know the importance of putting into practice the principle of giving love and the principle of self-improvement, which is to know yourself, know your true nature, and work to refine your true self towards enlightenment.

Utopia — Bringing Heaven to Earth

We need to turn Earth into an ideal world, a Utopia, by using the two important tools of love and enlightenment. This Utopia does not focus on the acquisition of material wealth. I have no intention of criticizing the convenience of this world any more than I would deny the importance of food, clothing, housing, or any other necessity of life. I am quite aware of the fact that the things of this world provide people with feelings of happiness. What I would like to say, however, is that we must not confuse things that are of primary importance with those that are of secondary importance.

Do not forget that spiritual refinement is the purpose of your life on Earth and is therefore of primary importance. We receive benefits from civilization and the conveniences of this world only to facilitate our spiritual refinement. Never mistake the theme for the subplot.

No matter what kind of society or lifestyle people have, it is important to build a society that focuses on the mind, where people see and strive for love and enlightenment. The sort of ideal world we are aiming to achieve is not necessarily one that is visible to the eye. Creating Utopia in this world does not infer we should have specific buildings, roads, political doctrines, or ways of life. These are variables that can easily change.

While living in a transient world, you have to be aware of what is eternal. You need to know the direction in which you should be heading and the heights at which to aim. Then you must work to bring this world to resemble the realms of the bodhisattvas and tathagatas, the world of angels. This is why numerous people strive for spiritual refinement for many, many years in this world through the cycles of reincarnation. This is God's great plan.

In comparison with what we learn at school and in society, what I have been telling you might seem absurd. But when you leave this world and return to the next one, you and every other person will discover that my words are 100 percent true. You might ask, "If we are going to discover this after death, why not simply leave it until then?" But it is best that every one of you realizes this Truth at the earliest opportunity.

I would like to help the people living in this world so that they do not have to spend several hundred years suffering in the darkness of Hell after they die. There are most certainly incorrect ways of living, so it is necessary to inform others if they are making mistakes, and to help them to live in the right way. This is what angels in Heaven do; it is their job. But it is also part of our duty to do what we can on Earth. Rather than people having to suffer after death, it is our duty to pass on what we know while they are still living in this world.

The driving force that is required, to create an ideal world on Earth, comes from conveying the Truth to others. Doing so is an act of love. If more and more people believe, the time will come when the power of our faith reaches a level at which everyone accepts our beliefs as the Truth. To hasten the coming of this day, I hope that this book will find its way into the hands of as many people as possible and become a guide for those who have not yet awakened to their full potential. I pray that all who read this book will take its lessons to heart and begin to live the Truth as children of God.

About the Author

IN 1981, MASTER RYUHO OKAWA started receiving messages from great historical figures—Jesus, Buddha, and others from Heaven. These holy beings came to him with impassioned messages of urgency, entreating him to deliver their holy wisdom to people on Earth. His calling to become a spiritual leader, to inspire people all over the world with the long-hidden spiritual Truths of the origin of humankind and the soul, was revealed. These conversations unveiled the mysteries of Heaven and Hell, and became the foundation on which Master Okawa built his spiritual philosophy.

As his spiritual awareness deepened, he understood that the wisdom he received has the power to help mankind overcome religious and cultural conflicts, and usher in an era of peace and harmony on Earth. Just before his thirtieth birthday, Master Okawa resolved to leave his promising career in business and dedicate himself to publishing the messages he received from Heaven. Since then, he has become a best-selling author in Japan, publishing more than 600 books. The universality of the wisdom he shares, the all-encompassing unity of his religious and spiritual philosophy, delivered in his uniquely simple and pragmatic method, attracts hundreds of millions of readers. In addition to his ongoing writing, Master Okawa gives public talks and lectures throughout the world.

About Happy Science

In 1986, Master Ryuho Okawa founded Happy Science, a spiritual movement dedicated to bringing greater happiness to humankind through overcoming barriers of race, religion, and culture and working toward an ideal united world of peace and harmony. Supported by followers who live by Master Okawa's words of enlightened wisdom, Happy Science has grown rapidly since its beginnings in Japan and now extends throughout the world. Today, it has more than 10 million members around the globe, with faith centers in major cities, including New York, Los Angeles, San Francisco, Tokyo, London, Sydney, São Paulo, and Seoul, among many others.

Master Okawa gives weekly talks at Happy Science centers and travels around the world giving public lectures. Happy Science provides various programs and services to support local communities and people in need. These include preschools, after-school educational programs for youth, and services for senior citizens and the disabled. Members also participate in social and charity activities, which in the past have included providing relief aid to earthquake victims in Chile and China, raising funds for a charity school in India, and donating mosquito nets to hospitals in Uganda.

Check out our Welcome e-booklet at:

www.happyscience-usa.org/introduction.html
(or click on the booklet on the happyscience-usa.org home page)

Programs and Events

Happy Science faith centers offer regular events, programs, and seminars. Join our meditation sessions, video lectures, study groups, seminars, and book events. Our programs will help you:

- Deepen your understanding of the purpose and meaning of life
- Improve your relationships as you learn how to love unconditionally
- Learn how to calm your mind even on stressful days through the practice of contemplation and meditation
- Learn how to overcome life's challenges … *and much more*

International Seminars

Each year, friends from all over the world join our international seminars, held at our faith centers in Japan. Different programs are offered each year and cover a wide variety of topics, including improving relationships, practicing the Eightfold Path, and loving yourself, to name just a few.

Happy Science Monthly

Read Master Okawa's latest lectures in our monthly booklet, *Happy Science Monthly*. You'll also find stories of members' life-changing experiences; news from Happy Science members around the world; and in-depth information about Happy Science movies, book reviews, and much more.

Available in English, Portuguese, Spanish, French, German, Chinese, Korean, and other languages. Back issues are available upon request. Subscribe by contacting the Happy Science location nearest you.

Contact Information

Happy Science is a worldwide organization with faith centers around the globe. For a comprehensive list of centers visit *Worldwide Directory* at **www.happyscience-usa.org**.

The following are a few of the many Happy Science locations:

UNITED STATES

New York
79 Franklin Street, New York, NY 10013
Phone: 212-343-7972 • Fax: 212-343-7973
Email: ny@happy-science.org
Website: www.happyscience-ny.org

Los Angeles
1590 E. Del Mar Boulevard, Pasadena, CA 91106
Phone: 626-395-7775 • Fax: 626-395-7776
Email: la@happy-science.org
Website: www.happyscience-la.org

San Francisco
525 Clinton Street, Redwood City, CA 94062
Phone/Fax: 650-363-2777
Email: sf@happy-science.org
Website: www.happyscience-sf.org

INTERNATIONAL

London

3 Margaret Street, London W1W 8RE, UK
Phone: 44-20-7323-9255 • Fax: 44-20-7323-9344
Email: eu@happy-science.org
Website: www.happyscience-eu.org

Tokyo

1-6-7 Togoshi, Shinagawa, Tokyo 142-0041
Japan
Phone: 81-3-6384-5770 • Fax: 81-3-6384-5776
Email: tokyo@happy-science.org
Website: www.kofuku-no-kagaku.or.jp/en

Other Books by Ryuho Okawa

The Laws of the Sun: Discover the Origin of Your Soul

The Golden Laws: History through the Eyes of the Eternal Buddha

The Laws of Eternity: Unfolding the Secrets of the Multidimensional Universe

The Starting Point of Happiness: A Practical and Intuitive Guide to Discovering Love, Wisdom, and Faith

Love, Nurture, and Forgive: A Handbook to Add a New Richness to Your Life

An Unshakable Mind: How to Overcome Life's Difficulties

The Origin of Love: On the Beauty of Compassion

Invincible Thinking: There Is No Such Thing as Defeat

Guideposts to Happiness: Prescriptions for a Wonderful Life

The Laws of Happiness: The Four Principles for a Successful Life

Tips to Find Happiness: Creating a Harmonious Home for Your Spouse, Your Children, and Yourself

The Philosophy of Progress: Higher Thinking for Developing Infinite Prosperity

The Essence of Buddha: The Path to Enlightenment

The Challenge of the Mind: A Practical Approach to the Essential Buddhist Teaching of Karma

The Challenge of Enlightenment: Realize Your Inner Potential

The Science of Happiness: 10 Principles for Manifesting Your Divine Nature